Excel 2024

Excel 2024: From Beginner to Expert in 7 Days with a comprehensive, illustrated guide covering all functions and formulas with simple, clear examples.

Alan Dinkins

© Copyright 2023-2024 by [Alan Dinkins] - All rights reserved.

The following Book is reproduced below with the goal of providing information that is as accurate and reliable as possible. Regardless, purchasing this Book can be seen as consent to the fact that both the publisher and the author of this book are in no way experts on the topics discussed within and that any recommendations or suggestions that are made herein are for entertainment purposes only. Professionals should be consulted as needed prior to undertaking any of the action endorsed herein.

This declaration is deemed fair and valid by both the American Bar Association and the Committee of Publishers Association and is legally binding throughout the United States.

Furthermore, the transmission, duplication, or reproduction of any of the following work including specific information will be considered an illegal act irrespective of if it is done electronically or in print. This extends to creating a secondary or tertiary copy of the work or a recorded copy and is only allowed with the express written consent from the Publisher. All additional right reserved.

The information in the following pages is broadly considered a truthful and accurate account of facts and as such, any inattention, use, or misuse of the information in question by the reader will render any resulting actions solely under their purview.

There are no scenarios in which the publisher or the original author of this work can be in any fashion deemed liable for any hardship or damages that may befall them after undertaking information described herein.

Additionally, the information in the following pages is intended only for

informational purposes and should thus be thought of as universal. As befitting its nature, it is presented without assurance regarding its prolonged validity or interim quality. Trademarks that are mentioned are done without written consent and can in no way be considered an endorsement from the trademark holder.

Table of Contents

Chapter 1: Kickstart Your Excel Journey: The Basics for Newbies 9

Chapter 2: Navigating the Excel Universe: The Interface Explained 13

Chapter 3: Speaking Excel: Mastering the Terminology 23

Chapter 4: Lightning Fast Excel: Essential Keyboard Shortcuts 29

    Excel worksheet navigation shortcuts: 30

    Shortcuts on worksheets and for formatting cells: 31

    Shortcuts for doing basic things in Excel: 33

    Excel shortcuts for doing math: 34

    Excel tools for formulas and functions for people just starting out: 35

    Shortcuts in Excel that use the CTRL key: 36

    Shortcuts in Excel that use the SHIFT key: 38

    Shortcuts in Excel that use the ALT key: 40

Chapter 5: The Power of Formulas and Functions in Excel 44

    Basic functions and formulas to know in Excel: 44

    Other types of Excel functions 52

    Statistical Functions: 53

Chapter 6: Unveiling Data Stories: Analyzing Data in Excel 56

    Sorting Data 59

    Filtering Data 60

    Data Validation 61

    Data Cleaning: 61

    Analysis of "What If" 63

    Goal Seeking 64

Chapter 7: Visualizing Data Brilliance: Using Charts in Excel 66

    How to create a Chart in Excel 2024 67

    Most used charts in excel 2024 70

Chapter 8: Organize Like a Pro: Tables in Excel 76

    Understanding Why and How Tables Are Useful 76

Everything you need to know about tables in excel 2024 77

Pivot tables user manual 80

Chapter 9: Pitfall Patrol: Common Mistakes to Avoid in Excel 86

Misinterpretation of Formulas and Functions 86

Inadequate Validation of Data 87

Poor Worksheet and File Organization.. 88

Common Errors in Excel 89

Pitfalls in Cell Merging, Non-Tabular Layout, Date Formatting, External Links, Formatting Whole Columns/Rows, Multiple Records in One Cell, and File Types 90

Chapter 10: Excel Wizardry: Uncover Advanced Tricks 94

Adding a drop-down list 94

How to Put Together Text with "&" 95

Hiding Formulas 96

Keeping information secret 96

Transposing Values... 97

Putting in numbers that start with 0 98

Use Excel's Wildcard Character to do a broad search 98

Using Data Validation to put limits on what can be typed in...................................... 99

One click is all it takes to get more status 100

Time-Saving Templates 101

Conclusion: Life's Solutions, Excel Style: Solve Everyday Problems with Excel........ 102

Learn How to Improve Personal Finances 102

Excel's Impact on Lives and Careers... 106

Chapter 1: Kickstart Your Excel Journey: The Basics for Newbies

Dear Reader, welcome to your journey through the world of Excel 2024! This book is your map, your guide, and your friend as you go on this exciting journey. You might be asking, "Why Excel?" or "Why should I learn Excel 2024?" Excel is a powerful tool that can help you make sense of data, solve hard problems, and even make better choices in your personal and professional life.

This book is made especially for people who have never used a computer before, let alone a complicated tool like Excel. Don't worry if you feel like you have too much to do! All of us have been there. It can be scary to learn a new skill, especially one that involves technology. But keep in mind that everyone was once a newbie.

Our plan in this book is simple: we're going to take things one step at a time. We'll start with the basics, like what Excel is and why it's useful. Then, we'll slowly move on to more difficult topics, such as formulas, functions, and data analysis. We'll give you clear explanations of each idea and lots of examples to help you understand and use what you've learned.

The goal is that by the end of this book, you'll be able to use Excel 2024 with ease, manipulate data well, and build your own Excel worksheets with confidence. This should be possible in just seven days. You'll go from knowing nothing about Excel to being an Excel expert with the information and skills to use it in many different ways.

So, are you ready to begin this exciting adventure? Are you ready to find out how to use Excel 2024 to its fullest potential? If you said yes, then let's jump in together!

Microsoft Excel, which is often just called Excel, is a powerful spreadsheet tool that is part of the Microsoft Office suite. A spreadsheet is basically a digital grid of cells that are set up in columns and rows. Every cell can hold different types of data or a formula that uses the data to do calculations.

Excel works best with numbers and statistics, but it can also handle text, dates, and a wide range of other types of data. You can type data into these cells by hand, or you can import data from databases or other files.

Once the data is in Excel, there are many ways to change it. You can sort and select the data, change its format, and use it in calculations. Excel's strength is that it can quickly and accurately do complicated calculations and analyses on a large amount of data. For example, you can use Excel to figure out the sum, average, or maximum of a group of numbers, or you can use more complicated statistical or financial functions.

Excel also lets you make formulas that use the information in your worksheet to do calculations. These methods can be as simple as adding and taking away, or they can be more complicated and involve statistical, financial, or logical calculations.

Excel is used in almost every business and job. Accountants use it to track financial transactions and make reports, scientists use it to analyze lab results, and students use it to keep track of their grades. It's a flexible tool that can help you organize and understand data, which makes it easier to make smart choices.

Let's talk about Excel in the year 2024. In this book, we'll be focused on this version of Excel. Excel 2024 keeps the main features of earlier versions, but adds a number of changes and new features that make it even more powerful and easy to use.

One of the best new things about Excel 2024 is its ability to analyze data in a more advanced way. It has new and better functions and features that make it easier and faster to analyze a lot of data. For example, it has better choices for conditional formatting, better tools for sorting and filtering, and stronger PivotTables for summarizing and analyzing data.

Excel 2024 works better with other Microsoft tools as well. This means that you can simply import data from or export data to other Microsoft programs like Word or PowerPoint. If you use OneDrive or SharePoint, you can also work with others on Excel workbooks in real time, which is a big plus in today's collaborative work settings.

Lastly, Excel 2024 has a user design that is easier to understand. The menu at the top of the Excel window, called the Ribbon, has been changed to make it easier to find and use the tools and functions you need. It also has a Quick Access Toolbar and a progress bar that you can change to fit your way of working.

With these changes, Excel 2024 is a better tool for analyzing data and easier to use, even for people who have never used it before. By the end of this book, you'll know everything you need to know to use Excel 2024 to its fullest.

Excel is a very useful tool in the business world. It can be used to keep track of sales, keep an eye on costs, figure out profits, look at trends, and do a lot more. A small business owner might use Excel to track their goods, while a marketing manager might use it to look at how well a campaign did. You can make it easier to understand and show your data by automating tasks, visualizing data, and making reports with Excel.

As we learn more about Excel, you'll see that it's not just a business tool. It's also a useful tool for people to use on their own. You can use Excel to keep track of your fitness progress, plan events, handle your budget, and even make games. There are a lot of options, and by the end of this book, you'll have the skills and information to use Excel 2024 to its fullest.

In the next lesson, we'll learn more about how to use Excel. You will learn how to move around in Excel and use its basic tools. We'll go over everything you need to know to get started, from starting a new workbook to putting data into cells. You'll be able to use Excel with ease and confidence by the end of the next lesson.

Don't forget that you're just getting started with Excel. There is a lot to learn, but don't worry, we'll take it step by step. Before you know it, you'll be a pro at using Excel. So let's keep going on this trip together. Stay tuned for the next part!

Chapter 2: Navigating the Excel Universe: The Interface Explained

Only the first step is to understand what Excel is and what it can do. The next important step is to dig deeper and learn more about Excel. This part will help you find your way around the Excel interface by explaining the workspace, the Ribbon, worksheets, workbooks, and basic operations. By the end of this part, you'll be able to move around in Excel with ease and confidence.

Think of the Excel office as the control center of a spaceship. You'll spend most of your time here, and it's where everything happens. The workspace is divided into different parts, each of which has its own job. At the top, you'll find the Quick entry Toolbar, which is a customizable area where you can put the commands you use most often for easy entry. Below it is the Ribbon, which is a set of tabs that group orders that are similar. For example, the 'Home' tab has commands for common jobs like copying and pasting, while the 'Insert' tab lets you add things like charts and tables to your worksheets.

The Ribbon: The Ribbon is an important part of how Excel works. It's where you'll find all the tools you need to change your info. Each tab on the Ribbon has a group of orders that all work together. For instance, the "Font" group on the "Home" tab has instructions for changing the font, size, color, and style of your text. The Ribbon also changes based on the job you're doing. This means that it changes the commands it shows you based on what you're doing. For example, if you choose a chart, the Ribbon will show you a group of "Chart Tools" that you can use to change and style your chart.

How to use the controls on the multifunction bar: The controls for all of Excel's functions are on the multifunction bar, which is also called the Ribbon. Depending on what they do, these tools are put into tabs and groups. For example, the 'Insert' tab has options for adding tables, charts, and shapes.

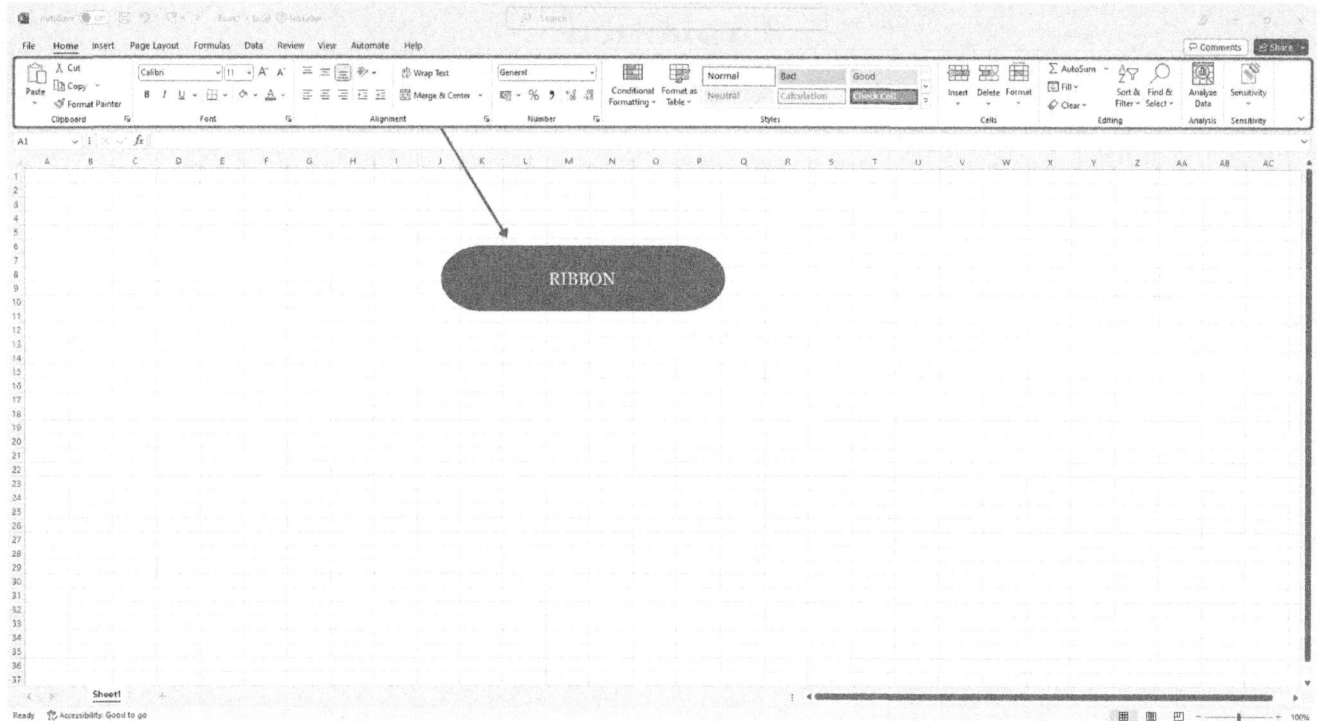

Changes to the Ribbon's look: In Excel 2024, the Ribbon has been given a new look that is cleaner and easier to use. You can now find and use the tools you need more easily. You can also customize the Ribbon by adding or removing tabs and actions from the tabs.

Quick Access Toolbar: The Quick Access Toolbar is at the top of the Excel screen, above the Ribbon tab. It makes it easy to get to tools like Save, Undo, and Redo that you use often. You can change the Quick Access Toolbar to include the tools you use most often.

Workbook view: The Workbook view is where you do most of your data manipulation. The Ribbon, the Formula Bar, and the Worksheet grid are all part of it. You can switch between different views of your file, such as Normal, Page Layout, and Page Break Preview, by clicking on the "View" tab on the Ribbon.

Formula bar: The Formula Bar shows the data or formula in the current cell. It is located above the Worksheet grid. You can add or change data or formulas in a cell by using the Formula Bar.

Worksheet grid: This is the main place where you work with data. It is made up of columns (called "column names") and rows (called "row names"). A cell is where a column and a row meet. It can hold either data or a formula.

Status bar: The Status Bar is at the bottom of the Excel interface. It shows the current mode, how many cells are chosen, and the average, count, or sum of the values in those cells. You can change the Status Bar to show different things.

Cells: A chart is made up of cells, which are its main building blocks. Each cell is named by the letter of its column and the number of its row, like A1, B2, etc. You can enter data or a formula into a cell.

Selection of cells, columns, and rows: To choose a cell, click on it. To choose a row, click on its row number. To choose a column, click on its letter. By clicking and dragging, or by holding down the Shift key and using the arrow keys, you can pick more than one cell, row, or column.

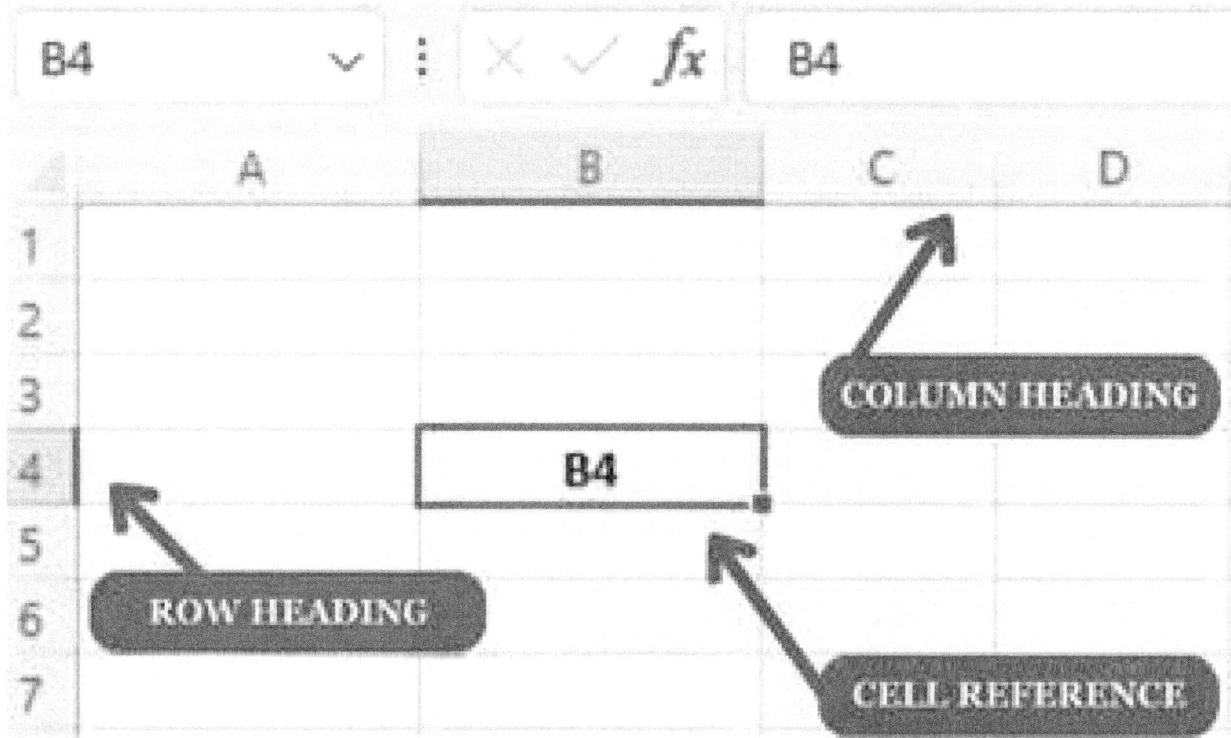

Inserting and removing: To insert a cell, row, or column, select the cell, row, or column you want to insert into and then choose the Insert command from the "Cells" group on the

"Home" tab. In the same way, you can delete cells, rows, or columns by picking them and then selecting the Delete command from the 'Cells' group on the 'Home' tab.

Formatting options: Excel lets you change the type, size, color, alignment, number format, and cell style of a cell, among other things. On the "Home" tab, you can find these choices in the groups called "Font," "Alignment," and "Number."

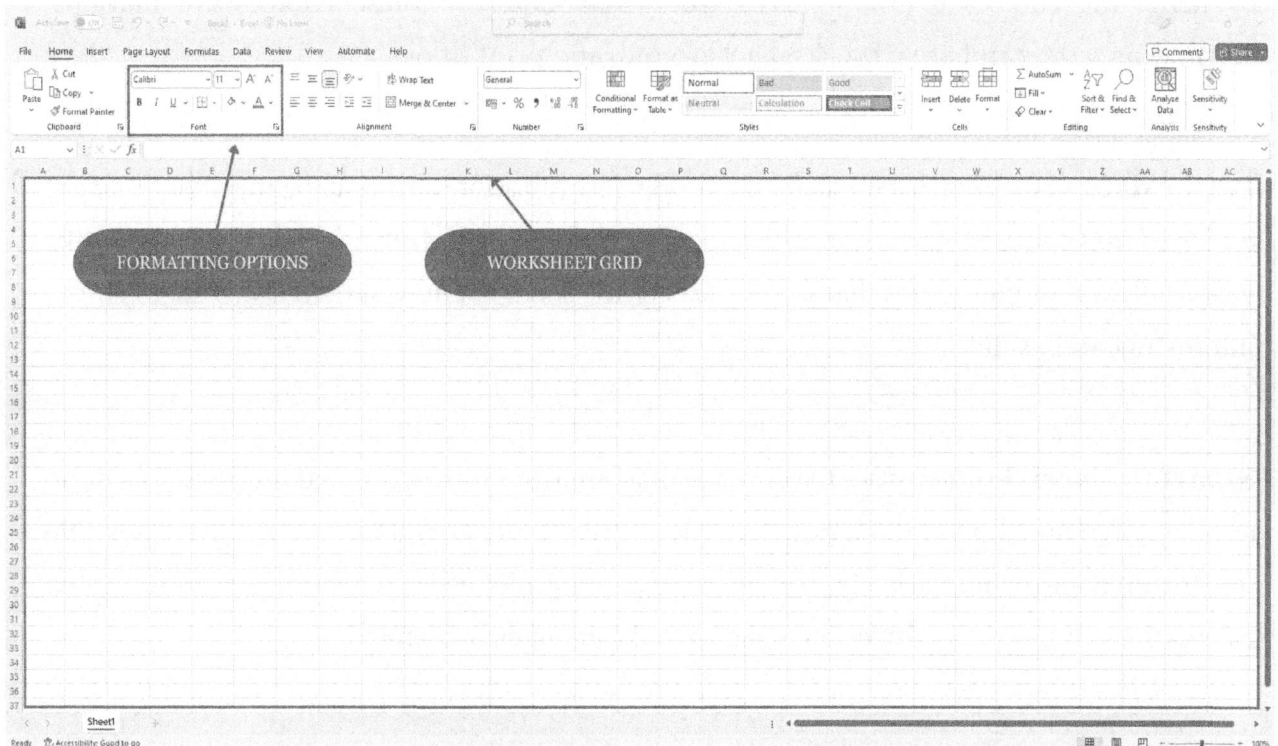

Formulas and functions: You can use formulas to do math with the information in your worksheet. Numbers, cell references, operators, and functions can all be used in a formula. Excel has a huge number of tools for different kinds of calculations, such as arithmetic, statistical, financial, and logical ones.

Sorting and filtering: You can sort data in ascending or descending order, by color, or by icon by using the Sort options in the "Sort & Filter" group on the "Data" tab. The 'sort' command in the 'Sort & Filter' group on the 'Data' tab can be used to sort data so that only rows that meet certain criteria are shown.

Accessing Contextual Menus: Excel's contextual menus make it easy to get to extra options and commands based on what you have chosen. You can open a contextual menu in Excel by right-clicking on a cell, column, row, or other feature. The menu that comes up will have commands and options that are related to the thing that was chosen. When you right-click on a cell, for example, you will see choices for formatting the cell, adding or removing cells, and doing calculations. Contextual menus make it easy to get to frequently used functions and can save you time that you would have spent looking for controls in the Ribbon.

Page layouts and printing: You can change how your worksheet looks when it's printed by using the choices on the "Page Layout" tab. Some of these choices are margins, orientation, size, print area, breaks, background, and print titles.

Better data visualization: Excel 2024 adds new tools for data visualization that make it easier to make charts, graphs, and dashboards that look good. It has new chart types like Waterfall and Funnel charts that make it easier for users to show data in a way that is more interesting and useful.

Smarter Excel Functions: Excel 2024 has smarter functions that make it easier to analyze large amounts of data. For example, the dynamic arrays feature makes it possible for formulas to automatically spread across multiple cells. This makes complicated calculations easier and reduces the need to make changes by hand.

Simplified Data Cleaning: Excel 2024 adds better tools for cleaning your data, which makes it easier to change and clean your data. Power Query lets you quickly load, clean, and change data from different sources, saving you time and effort in the process of getting the data ready.

Graphs and charts: Excel let you make many different graphs and charts to show your data clearly. You can make a chart by choosing the data you want to chart and then picking the type of chart you want from the "Charts" group on the "Insert" tab.

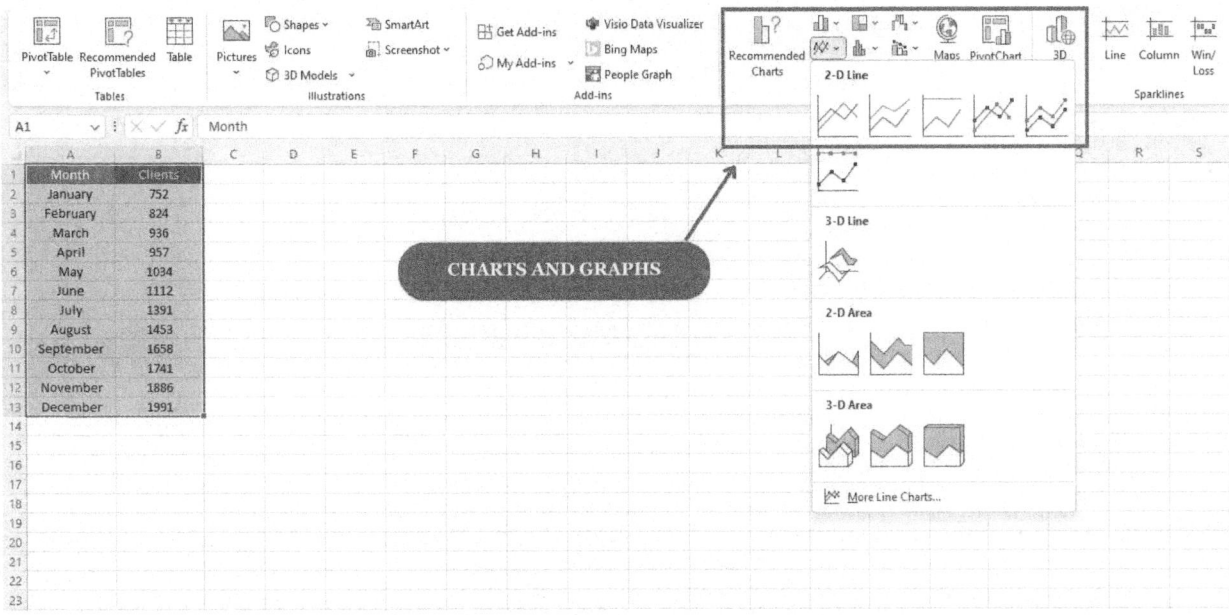

Accessibility is a top priority in Excel 2024, making sure that people with disabilities can use the software well. It has better support for screen readers, easier navigation with the keyboard, and other tools that make Excel more accessible.

If users are familiar with these core parts and how they work, they will be able to navigate Excel with confidence, structure and manage data easily, and use Excel's many features well. Once you understand these basics, you'll find that Excel is a powerful tool for analyzing, managing, and displaying data. When you understand these basic parts, you'll be on your way to becoming an Excel expert. You'll have the confidence to tackle complex data jobs and use all of Excel's features.

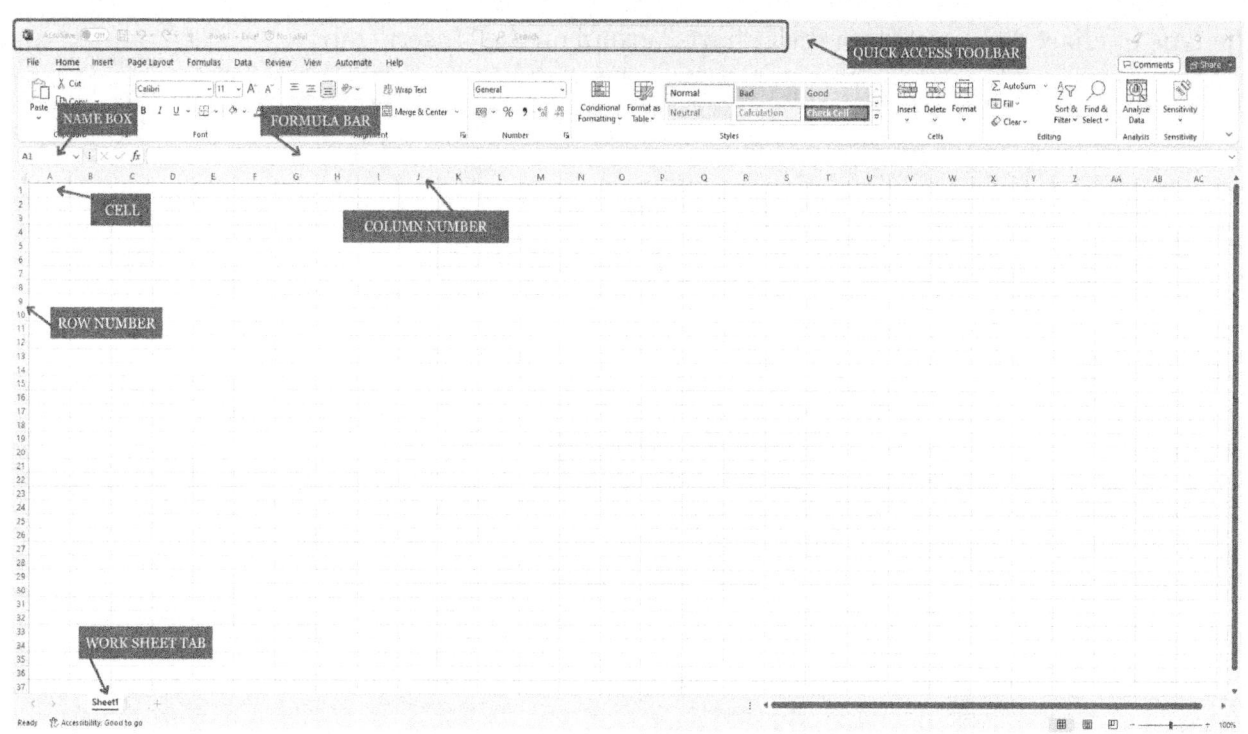

Chapter 3: Speaking Excel: Mastering the Terminology

In this section, we'll go over some basic terms that everyone who is just starting out with Excel 2024 should know. Learning the language is important because it makes it easier to communicate and work as a team in Excel. As you learn these terms, you'll be able to move around in Excel with confidence and use all of its many features.

First, let's break down some of the most important words you need to know:

Workbook: A file made in Excel is called a "workbook." Think of it like a book with many pages, and each page as a task. There can be more than one page in a workbook. For example, when making a budget, you could have one worksheet for each month, all of which would be kept in the same notebook.

Worksheet: This is a single page in an Excel file. It is made up of rows and columns of cells where you can put and change information. Take a budget chart as an example. It could have columns for different months and rows for different types of spending.

This is the smallest part of a page where information can be entered. It can be found by looking at where a row and a column meet, like A1, B2, and so on. For example, the amount planned for February's rent might be in cell B2.

Formula: This is an expression that uses the numbers in your worksheet to do calculations. It starts with an equal sign (=), then a mix of references to cells, operators, constants, and functions. For example, =B2+C2 would add up the numbers in cells B2 and C2.

Function: This is a set formula that does a specific calculation based on the information you give it. Excel has many different tools, such as SUM, AVERAGE, COUNT, and so on, that can be used for different kinds of calculations. For instance, the =SUM(B2:B12) method would add up all the numbers in cells B2 through B12.

Cell reference: This is the address of a cell on a worksheet, which is shown by the letter of the column and the number of the row, such as A1, B2, etc. For example, if you are writing a formula and need to refer to the number in the top left cell of the worksheet, you would use the cell reference A1.

Range: This is a group of cells that you choose for a certain action. It is shown by the cell references at the top left and bottom right, such as A1:B2. For example, you would use the range A1:B1 to add up all the numbers in the first two columns of the first row.

Formatting: Formatting means changing the way cells look so that the data is easier to read and looks better. It includes things like letter style, size, color, cell color, number format, and so on. For example, you could make the headers of your chart bold or use color formatting to draw attention to important values.

Sorting: Sorting means putting data in a certain order, either going up or down, based on a certain factor. For example, if you have a list of workers and their salaries, you could sort the list from highest salary to lowest salary to find out who makes the most.

Filtering: Filtering means showing only the data that fits a certain set of rules. This lets you focus on certain information in your dataset. For example, you could filter a list of employees to only show those who work in a certain area or make more than a certain wage.

Charts: Charts are pictures that show data. They make it easier to see patterns, trends, and differences in your data. For example, you could make a bar chart to compare how well different products sold or a line chart to show how sales have changed over time.

Pivot Tables: Pivot tables are powerful tools that allow you to quickly and easily summarize and examine large datasets. For example, if you have sales data for several different products over a number of years, you could use a pivot table to quickly figure out which product sold the most each year.

Form Controls: Form controls are interactive features like buttons, checkboxes, drop-down lists, etc. that you can add to your worksheets to make them more dynamic and user-friendly. You could, for example, add a checkbox that lets you show or hide certain rows of data or a drop-down list that lets you choose which data to show in a map.

Templates: These are Excel files that have already been made and can be used as a starting point for your own work. Formatting, formulas, and other elements that are often used for certain jobs are usually included. Excel, for example, has templates for budgets, invoices, calendars, and a number of other common chores.

AutoFill: AutoFill is a feature that quickly fills in cells with information that fits a pattern or is based on information in other cells. For example, if you type "January" in one cell and then use AutoFill to fill the next cells, Excel will instantly fill them with "February," "March," and so on.

Conditional Formatting: This feature lets you change how cells look based on what they contain. For example, you could use conditional formatting to automatically mark cells that have values above a certain limit or to color-code cells based on their values.

Freeze Panes: This feature lets you keep some rows or columns on the screen while you scroll through the rest of the page. For example, if you have a big worksheet with many rows, you could freeze the top row so that you can always see the headers as you scroll down.

Print Options: These are the choices that control how your worksheet will look when it is printed. For example, you can change the page orientation, margins, headers, footers, etc. For example, if your worksheet is wider than it is tall, you could set the page layout to landscape, or you could set the margins to a certain size to make sure all your data fits on the page.

Mastering Terms:

Like learning any new language, the best way to learn Excel terms is to use them often. Start by getting familiar with the words and what they mean. Then, as you do the tasks in this book, try to use these words to describe what you do. For example, instead of saying "I'm going to add these numbers together," you could say "I'm going to use the SUM function on this range of cells." With time, you'll know what to do when you hear these words. Keep in mind that it's fine to look back at this chapter or use online tools to help you remember the terms. The goal is to get used to the terms so that you can use them easily when you're working with Excel.

At this point, you know the basics of Excel's language, which is like learning the alphabet before you start putting together words and sentences. This new vocabulary you've learned is more than just a list of definitions; it's the language of Excel and the key to being able to use this powerful tool successfully.

Using the right words and making sure you understand them will help you in many ways.

Increasing Efficiency: Knowing what the different Excel tools do and how to use them will speed up your work and make you more efficient when using Excel. For example, if you know that the SUM function can quickly add up a group of numbers, you can skip adding each number by hand.

Boosting Confidence: If you learn the terms used in Excel, you'll feel more confident when working with the program. With your improved confidence, you might want to try out more advanced features and learn more.

Encouraging Collaboration: If you're on a team that uses Excel a lot, knowing the same terms can make it easier to talk to each other and work together. When everyone uses the same language, it's easier to explain how things work, share tips, and figure out what's wrong.

Making training easier: If you're going to teach others how to use Excel, you need to know what the terms mean. It not only helps you explain things correctly, but it also helps you answer questions in a clear way.

Helping You Solve Problems: When you have a problem with Excel, having the right words can speed up the process of finding a solution. You can do more effective searches online or use the help feature in Excel.

Preparing for Advanced Learning: If you want to take advanced Excel classes or get an Excel certification, you need to know the basic terms. It's a steppingstone to understanding more complex ideas and skills.

Excel is a tool that is used in many fields, so it can help you get a better job. Knowing the terms used in Excel can help you in job interviews and on the job. It might make it easier for you to get hired or get a raise.

In conclusion, learning the terms used in Excel is a good investment. It helps you understand Excel on a deeper level, so you can use all of its features to their full potential. With this knowledge, you'll be able to do tasks better and faster, which will make you a valuable asset in any job that needs Excel skills. So, keep studying, practicing, and learning more about Excel.

Chapter 4: Lightning Fast Excel: Essential Keyboard Shortcuts

Excel is a powerful tool, but its true potential can only be unlocked when you master the art of using shortcuts. Shortcuts are like secret passages in a castle, they get you where you need to go faster and more efficiently. They are combinations of keys that, when pressed together, perform a specific task within Excel. This chapter will introduce you to the world of Excel shortcuts, making your journey through Excel smoother and more efficient.

The importance of knowing and mastering Excel shortcuts cannot be overstated. They are the key to efficiency and speed in Excel. With shortcuts, you can perform tasks that would normally take several clicks with just a few keystrokes. This not only saves time but also reduces the risk of errors. The more you use these shortcuts, the more ingrained they become in your muscle memory, making their use second nature. Practicing these shortcuts regularly is the best way to master them.

As a novice, you should know a few important ways to save time. Some of the most important ones are Ctrl+C to copy, Ctrl+V to paste, and Ctrl+Z to undo. But Excel has a lot of other shortcuts that can make your job even easier. For example, if you want to add up the numbers in a column, you can just press Alt+= and Excel will add an SUM function for you. Or, you can press Alt+Enter to start a new line inside the same cell. These shortcuts are just the tip of the iceberg. As you learn more about Excel, you'll find many more that will speed up and simplify your work.

Excel worksheet navigation shortcuts:

Ctrl+Page Up: With this computer shortcut, you can move to the sheet before the one you're on. It's an easy way to switch between sheets when you're working with more than one.

Ctrl+Page Down: This shortcut lets you move to the next sheet in your spreadsheet. It works the same way as Ctrl+Page Up. It makes it easy to move between sheets without using the mouse.

Ctrl+Home: When you press Ctrl+Home, you go right to the beginning of the page, to cell A1. It's a quick way to get back to the point where your info started.

Ctrl+End: With this method, you can go to the last cell in the worksheet that has data in it. It makes it easy to find the end of your info quickly, especially when you're working with a lot of it.

Ctrl+Arrow Key (Up/Down/Left/Right): You can move to the edge of the current data area in the worksheet by pressing Ctrl and any arrow key. This is helpful for quickly moving through your info.

Alt+Page Up: Pressing Alt+Page Up changes your view in a worksheet one screen to the left. It lets you scroll across the screen to see information that isn't directly on the screen.

Alt+Page Down: On the other hand, Alt+Page Down moves your view in a page one screen to the right. It's useful for horizontal scrolling to see info to the right of where you are now.

Ctrl+Tab: If you have more than one open spreadsheet, Ctrl+Tab lets you switch to the next one. It's a quick way to move between different files without having to use the mouse.

Ctrl+Shift+Tab: In the same way, Ctrl+Shift+Tab lets you switch to the last open file if you have more than one open. It makes it easy to switch between your open files.

With Alt+Shift+F1, you can quickly add a new worksheet to Excel. It gives you an easy way to add more sheets to your notebook quickly.

Shift+F11: Inserts a new tab in Excel, just like Alt+Shift+F1. It's another way to add a sheet to your workbook fast.

Ctrl+F6: If you have more than one worksheet window open, you can use Ctrl+F6 to switch to the next one. It helps you move from one workbook window to another without using the mouse.

Ctrl+Shift+F6: On the other hand, when you have more than one workbook window open, Ctrl+Shift+F6 lets you switch to the previous workbook window. It is a quick way to switch between your open workbook files.

Ctrl+G: If you press Ctrl+G, the "Go To" menu box will open in Excel. This text box lets you type in a cell reference or a range address to go to a certain place in your worksheet. It makes it easier to get to a certain place quickly.

Excel's "Go To" box can also be opened with F5. It lets you quickly type in a cell reference or range address and jump to that place in your file.

Shortcuts on worksheets and for formatting cells:

Ctrl+C: When you press Ctrl+C in Excel, you can copy the chosen cells. This action copies the chosen data to the clipboard so you can paste it somewhere else in your worksheet or even in a different program.

Ctrl+X: Pressing Ctrl+X is a quick way to cut the cells that have been chosen. Like copying, cutting takes the chosen data from where it was and puts it in the clipboard so that it can be pasted somewhere else.

Ctrl+V: After copying or cutting cells, you can use Ctrl+V to put the copied or cut data somewhere else. This move adds the information from the clipboard to the cells that have been chosen.

Ctrl+Z: If you press Ctrl+Z, you can undo the last thing you did in Excel. This is helpful if you make a mistake and want to get your paper back to how it was before.

Ctrl+Y: In Excel, Ctrl+Y is the short cut for restart. When you press Ctrl+Y after undoing an action, the action you just undid is applied again, bringing back any changes you made.

Ctrl+A: When you press Ctrl+A, all the cells in the present worksheet are selected. This is a quick way to select all the data in your worksheet and work with it at once.

Ctrl+I: Pressing Ctrl+I gives the chosen cells an italic style. Text is often put in italics to make it stand out or to show that it is a title or heading.

Ctrl+U: Pressing Ctrl+U is a quick way to make the chosen cells stand out. Another way to draw attention to something on your paper is to underline it.

Ctrl+5: Pressing Ctrl+5 adds or removes the strikethrough style from the cells that have been chosen. People often use a strikethrough to show that a piece of information is no longer important or has been taken out.

Ctrl+P: Pressing Ctrl+P brings up the Print dialog box, where you can choose how to print your file and start the process. This lets you choose how you want to print, like how many copies you want, how the pages are oriented, and what size paper you want to use.

Ctrl+S: The short cut to save the file is Ctrl+S. If you press this key combination, any changes you make to the current file will be saved. It is best to save your work often so that you don't lose info.

Ctrl+O: Pressing Ctrl+O brings up the start dialog box, which lets you find and start a workbook in Excel. This is helpful if you want to switch to a different file or keep working on one you've already saved.

When you press Ctrl+N in Excel, a new file is made. This opens a new file with no data, formulas, or charts in it. You can start from scratch to add data, formulas, or charts.

Ctrl + 1: Opens the Format Cells text box. This is the best way to format cells quickly because it lets you change every part of the formatting from one place.

Ctrl+B: Makes the chosen cells bold. This is a quick way to draw attention to something important.

Open the Fill Color menu by pressing Alt+H+H. This lets you change the color of the background of the chosen cells.

Alt+H+B: Open the Border options. This lets you change or add a border to the chosen cells.

Shortcuts for doing basic things in Excel:

Ctrl+F: Find and replace. This is helpful if you want to find a certain piece of information in your paper or change some information to something else.

Ctrl+H: Replace. This works together with the Find command.

Ctrl+G: Means "Go To." This lets you get to a certain cell or range in your worksheet fast.

F7: Spell check. This will help you find any mistakes in your paper.

F12: Is Save As. This lets you save the current workbook under a new name or somewhere else.

Ctrl+N: Start a new book. This is how you start a new project in Excel.

Excel shortcuts for doing math:

F2: Change the current cell. This lets you change the formula or number in a cell right away.

Enter: Press Enter after typing a formula to figure it.

Ctrl+Enter: If you pick multiple cells and then enter a formula, Ctrl+Enter will put that formula into all the selected cells at once.

Ctrl+Shift+Enter: Instead of just pressing Enter, you'll need to press Ctrl+Shift+Enter when entering an array code.

F9: Add up all of the lessons in all of the open workbooks.

Shift+F9: The current worksheet is calculated.

Ctrl+Alt+F9: Calculates all files in all open workbooks, even if they've changed since the last time they were calculated.

Ctrl+Alt+Shift+F9: Rechecks formulas that depend on other formulas and then calculates all cells in all open files, even cells that aren't marked as needing to be calculated.

Ctrl+' (grave accent): Changes between showing cell numbers and formulas.

Alt+=: SUM() the chosen cells automatically.

Excel tools for formulas and functions for people just starting out:

This is the shortcut for the AutoSum function, which inserts the SUM function immediately.

Shift + F3: This brings up the Insert Function text box, which walks you through the steps of making a formula.

F4: After putting a cell reference (like 'B2') in a formula, press F4 to switch between relative and absolute references.

Ctrl+Shift+A: After you put the name of a function in a cell and add the opening parenthesis, this shortcut will add the syntax for the function arguments.

Tab: When you start typing the name of a function, Excel will show you a list of functions that start with the letters you've already written. You can use the arrow keys to choose the feature you want, and then press Tab to finish it.

Ctrl+Shift+U: Makes the formula bar bigger or smaller.

Ctrl+;: Put the current date in the cell that is active.

Ctrl+Shift+;: Add the current time to the cell that is currently selected.

Alt+M+V: This opens the "Evaluate Formula" text box, which lets you see step-by-step how Excel is figuring out your formula.

Alt+M+D: This brings up the "Add Watch" dialog box, which lets you keep an eye on the value of a certain cell while you work on another part of your spreadsheet.

When you are in a cell with a dropdown list, pressing Alt and the Down Arrow opens the list.

Ctrl+Shift+5: Use the style for percentages with no decimal places. This is helpful when the result of your math is a ratio or proportion.

Shortcuts in Excel that use the CTRL key:

Ctrl+D: You can fill down the chosen cells in Excel by pressing Ctrl+D. This action copies the content of the cell at the top of the range you chose and pastes it into the cells below.

Ctrl+R: The Excel key for filling to the right is Ctrl+R. It takes the information from the leftmost cell in the range you chose and puts it in the cells to the right.

Ctrl+K: When you press Ctrl+K in Excel, you can add a link. This is useful for making links to other files, websites, or specific places in the notebook that can be clicked on.

Ctrl+T: When you press Ctrl+T in Excel, the chosen cells become a table. Tables give you a structured way to manage and analyze data. They also have extra features like sorting, filtering, and formatting choices.

Ctrl+E: When you press Ctrl+E, Excel's Flash Fill tool is turned on. Flash Fill looks for patterns in your data and fills the rest of the cells based on those patterns. This is especially helpful when looking for specific information or organizing data in the same way every time.

Ctrl+Shift+L: The short cut for turning AutoFilter on and off in Excel is Ctrl+Shift+L. You can quickly sort columns in a dataset with AutoFilter, which lets you show only the data that meets certain criteria.

Ctrl+Shift+O: In Excel, selecting cells with notes is done by pressing Ctrl+Shift+O. This is helpful when you want to move quickly to cells with comments or do certain things to them.

Ctrl+Shift+Space: When you press Ctrl+Shift+Space in Excel, you can pick the whole worksheet. This picks all cells, rows, and columns in the active worksheet.

Ctrl+Shift+Right Arrow: When you press Ctrl+Shift+Right Arrow in Excel, you can pick the last cell in the current row. This is helpful when you want to quickly select a whole row of info.

Ctrl+Shift+Left Arrow: Ctrl+Shift+Left Arrow is used in Excel to go to the first cell of the current row. It lets you quickly choose a row of data from the current cell to the first cell in that row.

Ctrl+Shift+Up Arrow: In Excel, you can pick the first cell of the current column by pressing Ctrl+Shift+Up Arrow. This lets you quickly choose all the data in a column from the current cell to the top cell in that column.

Ctrl+Shift+Down Arrow: Pressing Ctrl+Shift+Down Arrow in Excel will take you to the last cell in the current column. This lets you quickly choose all the data in a column from the current cell to the last cell in that column.

Ctrl+Minus (-): In Excel, if you press Ctrl+Minus (-), the cells you have chosen will be deleted. This action deletes the text and formatting from the chosen cells.

Ctrl+Shift+Plus (+): The Excel method for adding a cell is Ctrl+Shift+Plus (+). It adds new cells within the range you chose, pushing down or to the right any current cells.

Ctrl+Shift+Colon (:): You can put the current time in a cell in Excel by pressing Ctrl+Shift+Colon (:). This adds the current time, including the hours, minutes, and seconds, immediately.

Ctrl+Shift+Double Quote ("): In Excel, you can copy the value from the cell above into the current cell by using Ctrl+Shift+Double Quote ("). This is helpful if you want to quickly copy a value.

Ctrl+Shift+Minus (-): In Excel, you can use Ctrl+Shift+Minus (-) to show any secret columns in the selection. This move makes columns that were hidden show up again.

Ctrl+Shift+Plus (+): In Excel, you can unhide any secret rows in the selection by pressing Ctrl+Shift+Plus (+). This move shows rows that were hidden, so they can be seen again.

Shortcuts in Excel that use the SHIFT key:

Shift + Space: In Excel, you can pick the whole row of the active cell by pressing Shift + Space. This is helpful when you want to change the way a whole row of data looks or do something with it.

Shift+Tab: When you use Shift+Tab in Excel, you can move to the previous cell. This is useful when you want to move backwards through the cells.

Shift+Right Arrow: When you press Shift+Right Arrow, the cell pick moves to the right.

It lets you quickly choose several cells to the right of the one you are currently working on.

Shift+Left Arrow: In Excel, Shift+Left Arrow moves the selection of cells to the left. It lets you choose various cells to the left of the one you're currently looking at.

Shift+Up Arrow: When you press Shift+Up Arrow, the cell pick moves up. This is helpful when you want to choose a group of cells above the ones you've already chosen.

Shift+Down Arrow: When you press Shift+Down Arrow in Excel, the cell selection moves down. It lets you choose more than one cell below the one you have chosen.

Shift+Page Up: When you use Shift+Page Up in Excel, the cell selection moves up one screen. This is helpful when you want to pick more cells than what you can see at the moment.

Shift+Page Down: When you press Shift+Page Down in Excel, the cell selection moves down one screen. It lets you choose more cells below the ones you can see at the moment.

Shift+Home: When you press Shift+Home in Excel, the cell selection goes to the beginning of the row. This is helpful when you want to pick all the cells from the current cell to the first cell in that row.

Shift+End: In Excel, Shift+End lets you pick the last cell in the current row. It lets you choose all the cells in that row from the current cell to the last one.

Shift+F11: If you press Shift+F11 in Excel, you can add a new tab. This adds a new page to your workbook quickly so you can use it to organize and analyze data.

Shift+F10: When you press Shift+F10, Excel shows the shortcut menu for the action you chose. This gives you a list of options and actions that are connected to the selected item. This makes it easy to do certain tasks quickly.

Shortcuts in Excel that use the ALT key:

Alt+H: When you press Alt+H, you can go to the Home tab on the Ribbon in Excel. This tab has the most frequently used tools for formatting and editing, like font styles, cell alignment, and tools for working with data.

Alt+N: With Alt+N, you can get to the Insert tab on the Ribbon in Excel. This tab gives you different ways to add new things to your paper, like tables, charts, pictures, and shapes.

Alt+P: If you press Alt+P in Excel, you can go to the Page Layout tab on the Ribbon. This tab lets you change how your printed worksheets look and how they are laid out. This includes page setup choices, headers and footers, and a print preview.

Alt+M: With Alt+M, you can get to the Formulas tab on the Ribbon in Excel. This tab has a variety of features and tools that you can use to work with formulas and do calculations in your worksheets.

Alt+A : When you press Alt+A, you can go to the Data tab on the Ribbon in Excel. This tab has tools for sorting, filtering, validating, and analyzing your data, as well as choices for managing and analyzing your data.

Alt+R : With Alt+R, you can get to the Review tab on the Ribbon in Excel. This tab has tools for reviewing your workbook and working together on it, such as spell check, track changes, comments, and choices for protecting it.

Alt+W : When you press Alt+W, you can go to the View tab on the Ribbon in Excel. This tab lets you change how you view and move around your workbook by giving you choices like zoom, gridlines, and window arrangement.

Alt+F1: With Alt+F1, you can quickly make a chart on a different Chart sheet from the data in the current range. This gives you a picture of your data, which makes it easy to analyze and present.

Alt+Shift+F1: You can add a new page to Excel by pressing Alt+Shift+F1. This adds a new sheet to your worksheet quickly so that you can use it to organize and analyze data.

Alt+Enter: When you type text in a cell, you can move to the next line in the same cell by pressing Alt+Enter. This is helpful when you want to add more than one line of text to a cell or make a line break.

Alt+Page Down : With Alt+Page Down, you can move to the right one screen in a form. This is helpful if you have a big paper and want to move around in the area you can see.

Alt+Page Up: When you press Alt + Page Up, you can move one screen to the left in a worksheet. This is helpful if you want to move left or right in a big worksheet's viewable area..

Alt+Tab: Pressing Alt+Tab allows you to quickly switch between open applications or windows on your computer. This is useful when you have multiple applications or windows open and need to switch between them efficiently.

You've now been introduced to a wide array of keyboard shortcuts that can help you navigate Excel 2024 with ease and efficiency. It might seem overwhelming at first, but remember, you don't need to memorize all of them right away. The key is to start with a few that you find most useful in your daily tasks and practice them until they become second nature. Then, gradually add more to your repertoire.

Remember, the beauty of Excel is that there are always multiple ways to accomplish any task. So, if you forget a shortcut, don't worry! You can still get the job done. But as you get more comfortable with these shortcuts, you'll find that they can significantly speed up your work and make the experience of using Excel more enjoyable.

Now, as we turn the page to Chapter 5, we're going to dive into one of the most powerful aspects of Excel: formulas and functions. These are the building blocks that allow Excel to perform calculations, analyze data, and automate tasks. So, take a deep breath, give yourself a pat on the back for mastering Excel shortcuts, and get ready to dive deeper into the world of Excel. The journey continues, and it only gets more exciting from here!

Chapter 5: The Power of Formulas and Functions in Excel.

Most of Excel's power comes from its functions and formulas. Even though these two words sound alike, they mean different things. A formula in Excel can be thought of as an equation that is used to do math on the numbers in a worksheet. A function, on the other hand, is basically a set formula that does a specific calculation. Using functions can help you simplify your models, making them easier to build and understand.

Let's dive into Excel's huge sea of functions and formulas and learn about some basic ones that every beginner should know.

Basic functions and formulas to know in Excel:

SUM: The SUM function is the one that all other Excel functions are built on. It looks at all the numbers in a set of cells and adds them all up. For example, if you have a list of costs in cells A1 through A10 and want to know how much they all add up to, you can use the SUM function. With the method =SUM(A1:A10), you could add up all the costs in cells A1 through A10. When working with bigger datasets, this is very helpful and saves time over adding each cell separately.

SUMIF:SUMIFS is an improved version of SUMIF that lets you add up cells that meet more than one condition. For example, the formula =SUMIFS(A1:A10, B1:B10, ">5", C1:C10, "10") adds up all the numbers in the range A1:A10 for which the number in column B is greater than 5 and the number in column C is less than 10.

	A	B	C
1	Country	Population	
2	China	1.389.618.778	
3	India	1.311.559.204	
4	USA	331.883.986	
5	Indonesia	264.935.824	
6	Pakistan	210.797.836	
7	Brazil	210.301.591	
8	Nigeria	208.679.114	
9	Russia	141.944.641	
10	Mexico	127.318.112	
11	SUM	=SUM(B2:B10)	output = 4.197.039.086

Formula bar: =SUM(B2:B10)

SUBTOTAL: This function can do different kinds of calculations on a range of cells, such as count, sum, average, maximum, minimum, etc. For example, =SUBTOTAL(1,A1:A10) will count how many cells from A1 to A10 have numbers in them, while =SUBTOTAL(9,A1:A10) will add up all the numbers from A1 to A10.

POWER: This function takes a number and multiplies it by a certain amount. For example, =POWER(2,3) will return 8, since 2 multiplied by 3 is 8.

TRIM: This tool gets rid of all the extra spaces in the text. For example, =TRIM("Hello World") will return "Hello World," without the extra spaces at the start and end.

CONCATENATE: This method combines two or more text strings into a single text string. For example, =CONCATENATE("Hello", ",", "World") will return "Hello World."

LEN: This method tells you how long a string of text is. For example, "Hello World" has 11 characters, so =LEN("Hello World") will return 11.

COUNT: The COUNT function counts how many cells in a specific range have numeric values in them. For example, you would use the COUNT method if you had a list of sales figures in cells B1 through B10 and wanted to know how many there were. With the formula =COUNT(B1:B10), you could find out how many cells from B1 to B10 have a number in them. This is very helpful when you need to figure out how many data points you have, like how many sales or survey answers you have.

	A	B	C
	B13	fx	=COUNT(B2:B12)
1	Country	Population	
2	China	1,389,618,778	
3	India	1,311,559,204	
4	Usa	331,883,986	
5	Indonesia	264,935,824	
6	Pakistan	210,797,836	
7		Empty	Skips non-numerical values
8	Brazil	210,301,591	
9	Nigeria	208,679,114	
10			Skips empty cells
11	Russia	141,944,641	
12	Mexico	127,318,112	
13	**COUNT**	=COUNT(B2:B12)	Output = 9
14			

COUNTIF and COUNTIFS: The COUNTIF function counts the number of cells that meet a single condition. The COUNTIFS function, on the other hand, counts the number of cells that meet more than one condition. For example, the formula =COUNTIF(A1:A10, ">5") counts the number of cells in the range A1:A10 that contain a number greater than 5. The formula =COUNTIFS(A1:A10, ">5", B1:B10, "10") counts how many cells in the range A1:A10 have a number greater than 5 and a number less than 10 in the matching cell in column B.

REPLACE : This code replaces a part of a text string with another text string. For example, =REPLACE("Hello World", 1, 5, "Goodbye") will return "Goodbye World" because it changes the first 5 characters of "Hello World" with "Goodbye."

SUBSTITUTE: This function swaps out current text in a text string with new text. For example, =SUBSTITUTE("Hello World", "World", "Excel") will return "Hello Excel" because it replaces "World" with "Excel."

UPPER, LOWER, and PROPER:UPPER turns text into all capital letters, LOWER into all lowercase letters, and PROPER into proper case, in which the first letter of each word is emphasized. For example, =UPPER("Hello World") will return "HELLO WORLD," =LOWER("Hello World") will return "hello world," and =PROPER("HELLO WORLD") will return "Hello World."

AND, OR: The AND function is a logical function that gives TRUE if all conditions are met and FALSE otherwise. On the other hand, if any of the conditions are met, the OR function will return TRUE. For example, if A1 is greater than 10 and B1 is less than 20, the formula =AND(A1>10, B1<20) gives TRUE. If either A1 or B1 is greater than 10 and less than 20, the formula =OR(A1>10, B1<20) returns TRUE.

INDEX and MATCH: You can use the INDEX and MATCH methods together to do lookups. The MATCH function finds the position of a given value within a range, while the INDEX function gets the value at a given position within a range. When used together, these lookup methods are more flexible than VLOOKUP and HLOOKUP because they don't have to look in the leftmost column or row and can handle both horizontal and vertical ranges. For example, the formula =INDEX(B1:B10, MATCH("Apple", A1:A10, 0)) will find where "Apple" is in cells A1:A10 and return the value from column B that goes

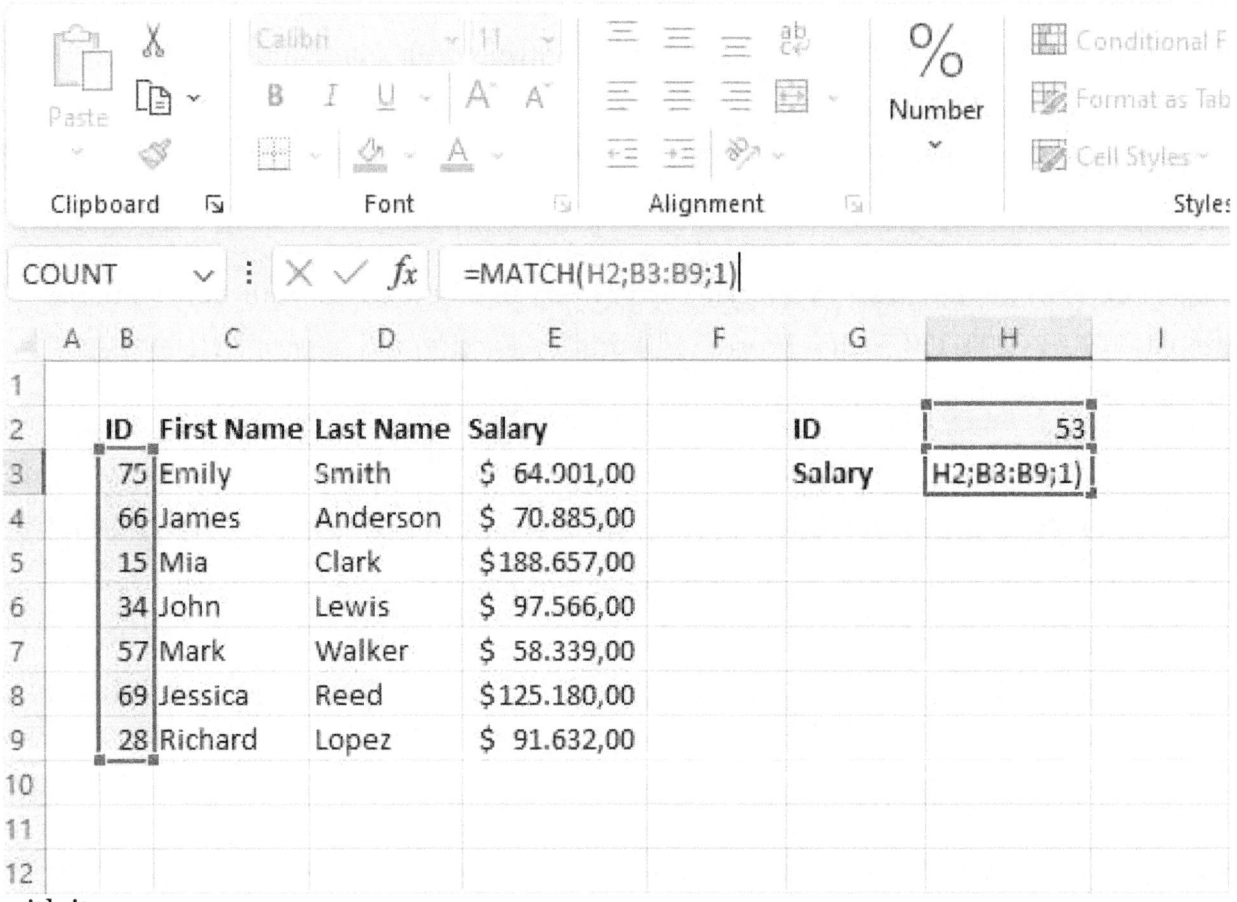

with it.

AVARAGE: The AVERAGE method figures out the average of a set of numbers. For example, you could use the AVERAGE function to find the average number from a list of test scores in cells C1 through C10. With the method =AVERAGE(C1:C10), all of the test scores from C1 to C10 are added together and then divided by the number of scores to get the average score. This is a quick and easy way to find the main trend in a set of data.

	A	B	C
	B11	=AVERAGE(B2:B10)	
1	Country	Population	
2	China	1.389.618.778	
3	India	1.311.559.204	
4	USA	331.883.986	
5	Indonesia	264.935.824	
6	Pakistan	210.797.836	
7	Brazil	210.301.591	
8	Nigeria	208.679.114	
9	Russia	141.944.641	
10	Mexico	127.318.112	
11	Average	=AVERAGE(B2:B10)	OUTPUT = 466.337.676
12			
13			

VLOOKUP: The VLOOKUP (Vertical Lookup) method is used to find information in a spreadsheet. This function looks down the leftmost column of the range you tell it to look at until it finds a number that matches the lookup value. Then, it gets information from a column you choose in the appropriate row. For example, you can use the VLOOKUP tool to find a student's name based on their ID number if you have a table with their ID numbers in column A and their names in column B. The method =VLOOKUP(12345, A1:B100, 2, FALSE) will look for the ID number 12345 in cells A1 through A100 and then return the name from column B.

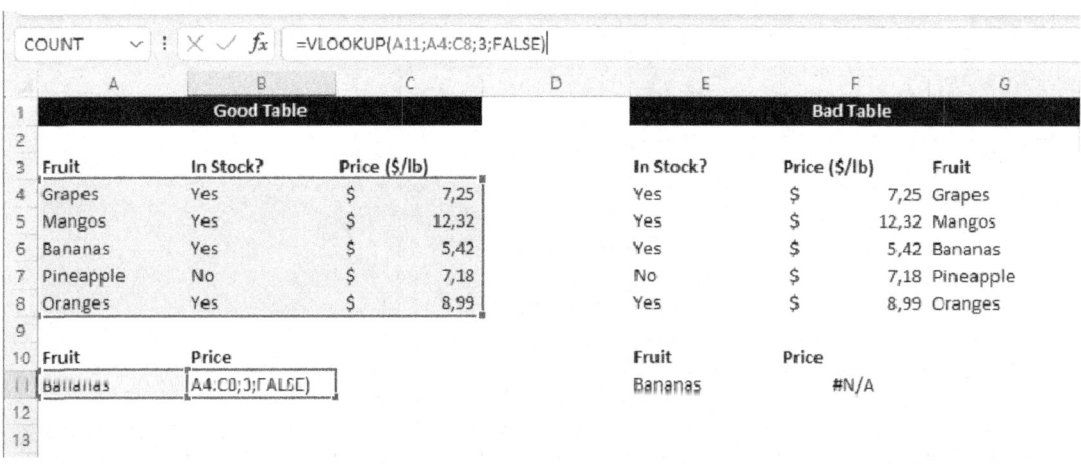

HLOOKUP: Like VLOOKUP, the HLOOKUP (Horizontal Lookup) function is used to find information in a spreadsheet, but it looks across the top row of a given range instead of down the column. For instance, if you have a table with the months in row 1 and the sales numbers for each month in row 2, you can use the HLOOKUP tool to find the sales numbers for a specific month. The formula =HLOOKUP("July", A1:L2, 2, FALSE) will look for the word "July" in cells A1 through L1 and return the sales number from row 2 if it finds it.

IF: The IF function in Excel lets you compare a number to what you expect based on what makes sense. In its most basic form, the IF function says: IF(Something is True, then do something, otherwise do something else). For example, you could use the IF function in a formula to figure out how much of a bonus to give salespeople who have reached a goal. If the sales number in cell A1 is 10,000 or more, the formula =IF(A1>=10000, "Bonus", "No Bonus") would return "Bonus," and if it is less than 10,000, it would return "No Bonus."

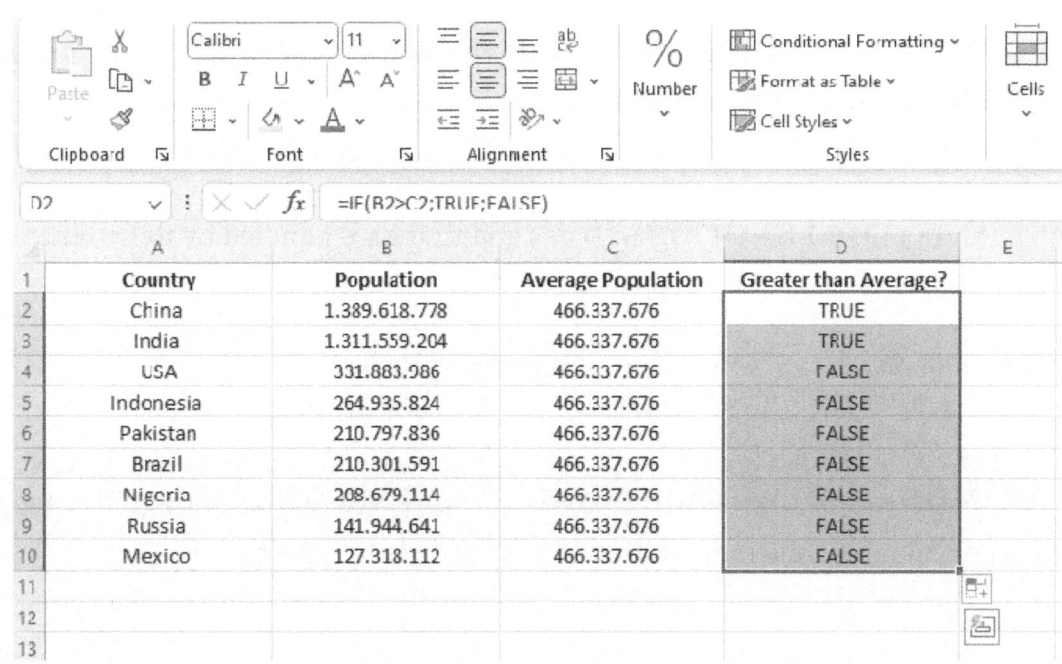

Here are some functions and formulas you can use in Excel, from the most basic to the most complicated. It's important to remember that each function and formula has its own syntax, which includes how to use brackets and commas correctly. Also, keep in mind that Excel functions don't care about case, so you can type them in all capital letters, all lowercase letters, or a mix of both.

Other types of Excel functions

In addition to the functions we've already talked about, there are also some other types of Excel functions.

TEXT FUNCTIONS: These functions let you work with text strings and change them.

LEFT, RIGHT, and MID: These methods are used to get a certain number of characters from the left, right, or middle of a text string.

DATE AND TIME FUNCTIONS: Dates and times are handled by these functions.

TODAY and **NOW** give you the current date and/or time.

YEAR, MONTH, DAY, HOUR, MINUTE, and SECOND: These functions give back the part of a date or time number that corresponds to that part.

EDATE and EOMONTH return the date that is a certain number of months before or after a given date.

LOOKUP AND REFERENCE FUNCTIONS: There are more tools than VLOOKUP, HLOOKUP, INDEX, and MATCH that can be used to find information in a spreadsheet.

OFFSET: This method returns a cell or range that is a certain number of rows and columns away from a given cell or range.

INDIRECT: This method gives back the reference that a text string tells it to.

Statistical Functions:

AVERAGE: This function finds the average (arithmetic mean) of a bunch of numbers.

This method gives back the statistical median, which is the number in the middle of a set of numbers.

MODE: This function gives back the number that shows up most often in a bunch of numbers.

STDEV and VAR: These methods figure out the standard deviation and variance, which show how far from the average something is.

Excel has over 400 built-in tools, so there are a lot more than just the ones on this list. Some of the most common ones are mentioned above, but you can find a function for almost any kind of calculation or data analysis task. If you need a function that Excel doesn't already have, you can also use Visual Basic for Applications (VBA) to make your own unique function.

Even though it may seem hard at first, know that it takes time to learn how to use these tools well. It's not as important to remember every tool as it is to know how they work and when to use them.

The best way to get used to these numbers and functions is to use them over and over again. Try making your own examples, or even better, use what you've learned on your own data. Don't be afraid to try new things and make mistakes, because that's how you learn. And don't forget that you can always use this chapter as a help.

As we go on, you'll see that these formulas and functions are the building blocks for more complicated data analysis. They will give you strong ways to manipulate and question your data, turning raw numbers into insights.

We'll take these skills to the next level in the next lesson. We'll look at how to use the tools and methods we've already learned to examine data in Excel. We'll look at how to sort and filter data, make pivot tables, and more.

Even though the number of tools may seem overwhelming at first, remember that it takes time to learn how to use them well. The goal isn't to memorize every single tool, but to understand how they work and figure out when and where to use them.

Doing practical tasks is the best way to learn these formulas and functions. Try coming up with your own examples or, better yet, use what you've learned on your own data sets. Don't be afraid to try new things and make mistakes. Both are important parts of the learning process. Also, you can always use this part as a point of reference.

As we go on, you'll see that these numbers and functions are the building blocks for more complex ways to analyze data. They will give you the power to change and look into your data in powerful ways, turning numbers into important insights.

In the next part, we'll take these skills to the next level. We'll use the tools and methods we've learned so far to look at data in Excel. We'll learn how to sort and group data, build pivot tables, and do other things.

Chapter 6: Unveiling Data Stories: Analyzing Data in Excel

Excel is more than just an app for making spreadsheets. It is a powerful and flexible tool that makes it easy for users to manage big amounts of data. When you put data into Excel, you're not just filling cells with information; you're making a dynamic database that lets you structure, change, and examine data.

Excel's real strength is that it can turn raw data into useful insights. It gives you a well-organized place to look for trends, patterns, and important information. Excel can do more with data analysis than specialized statistical tools could do.

As you add information to Excel, it becomes a thing that can be grouped, filtered, and looked at in different ways. This is when the data processing tools in Excel come in handy. All of these tools use Excel's familiar interface to let you do complicated calculations, statistical tests, visualizations, and more.

You don't have to know a lot about statistics to use Excel to examine your data well. It makes the process easier to understand and use, even for people who have never done it before. You can quickly filter data to focus on certain criteria, sort data to see how it is spread out, use math and functions to learn new things, and make charts and graphs to show what you've learned.

When working with large files, Excel's ability to analyze data is especially helpful. It lets you combine and summarize data based on different factors, make pivot tables for dynamic analysis, do regression analysis to figure out how things are related, and do scenario analysis to look into different options.

The best thing about Excel's tools for analyzing data is that they are easy to use. You don't have to be scared of statistics jargon or complicated ideas. Excel has step-by-step wizards and easy-to-use interfaces that walk you through the analysis process and give you the tools you need to make good choices based on the facts and insights your data gives you.

Putting data into Excel is one of the most important steps in analyzing data. Excel gives you different ways to enter data, so you can choose the one that works best for you. Let's figure out how to enter and handle data in Excel 2024 as quickly as possible.

Entering data by hand:

To add data by hand, click on the cell you want to use and start typing. Press the "Enter" key or use the arrow keys to move to the next cell. Excel instantly changes the width of a cell based on what's in it. For example, if you have a column called "Product Names," you can type the names of the goods right into the cells that go with them.

Copying and Pasting Data:

You can easily copy and paste data from a Word document, a site, or an email into Excel. Select the data in the source document, right-click, and choose "Copy" (or press "Ctrl+C"). Then, go to Excel and right-click on the cell where you want to put the data. To add the copied data to Excel, choose "Paste" (or press "Ctrl+V"). This method is helpful if you want to quickly move data from outside sources into Excel so you can analyze it.

Bringing in information from a file or database:

Excel permits you to import data from different file formats and databases. To import data, go to the "Data" tab on the Excel ribbon, click "Get Data," and then choose the right choice for importing based on where your data comes from. You can import information from a CSV file, an Excel file, an Access database, or even a website or SharePoint. Excel will help you through the import process by letting you choose the data you want and tell it how to organize it.

Once you have your data in Excel, you can use its built-in tools to do math and gain insights. Let's look at some of the most important functions that help you understand and study your data:

Figuring out the totals:

Excel's SUM tool is the only way to figure out how much a group of cells add up to. For instance, if you have a column of sales numbers, you can use the SUM tool to find out how much money was made during a certain time period. Just type "=SUM(" and the set of cells you want to add up (for example, "=SUM(A2:A10)") and press "Enter."

Averaging Data:

The AVERAGE function lets you find the average of a range of cells. For example, if you have a column of test scores, you can use the AVERAGE function to find the average score. Type "=AVERAGE(" followed by the range of cells (for example, "=AVERAGE(B2:B10)") and press "Enter."

How to Figure Out Percentages:

Excel's formulas make it easy to figure out percentages. For example, if you want to know how much each product's sales contributed to the total, you can use the formula "=Sales/Total Sales" and style the cell as a percentage.

Formatting based on conditions:

Excel's conditional formatting feature lets you highlight certain data points based on custom conditions. For example, you can highlight all sales figures above a certain threshold in green and those below the threshold in red. This makes it easier to see patterns and outliers in your data.

By putting these data entry techniques, important functions, and formatting tools together, you can get a full picture of your data. Don't forget to try out different formulas and functions to see what works best for your analysis.

If you know how to sort and filter in Excel, you can study and analyze your data in more depth. Whether you have a small set of data or a large one, Excel's intuitive tools make sorting and filtering your data easy.

Let's take a guided trip with real-world examples of how to sort and filter data in Excel 2024.

Sorting Data

Find the Data Range: Find the range of cells that contain the data you want to sort. This could be one column of data or more than one.

Find the Sort Settings: Go to the "Data" tab on the Excel toolbar and click the "Sort" button. A window will pop up to help you set the sorting settings.

Choose the Column to Sort: In the dialog box, choose the column you want to use to sort your data. For example, if you have a database of customer names and want to put them in alphabetical order, choose the column with the first letter of each name.

Choose the Sort Order: Depending on your needs, you can choose whether you want the order to go from A to Z or from Z to A.

Implement Multiple Sort Levels (If Needed): If your data spans multiple columns and you want to sort using multiple benchmarks, you can add extra levels of sorting. This lets you select and fine-tune the sorting order based on different columns.

Validate the Sorting Procedure: Click "OK" to start the sorting process. Excel will then reorganize the data based on your choices.

Filtering Data

Find the Data Range: Just like when you sort, you should start by finding the range of cells that hold your data.

Explore the Filter Settings: Click the "Filter" button on the "Data" tab of the Excel toolbar. This will add drop-down arrows to the title row of each column in your dataset.

To use the filter, tap the drop-down arrow in the column you want to filter. A list of filtering choices will appear, allowing you to sort the data based on certain criteria.

Set the Filter Standards: Set the filter standards for the chosen column. For example, in a sales dataset, if you want to see sales that are more than $1,000, you can change the filter to only show sales that are more than $1,000.

Use Multiple Filters (If Necessary): If your dataset has more than one column and you want to apply filters based on different factors at the same time, you can repeat the filtering process for each column.

Fine-tune the Filter Standards: Excel has advanced filtering choices, like filtering by color, text, or complex logical operators. Use these to make your filter conditions fit your needs.

By organizing and filtering your data, you can get important insights and focus on specific parts of your dataset. Excel's easy-to-use design and powerful features make it easy for beginners to manipulate and analyze data.

Validating and cleaning your data in Excel is important to keep it accurate, consistent, and trustworthy. These steps are also important for figuring out what your data means and making good decisions.

Data Validation

Select the Data Range: Find the range of cells where you want to enforce data validation. This could be a single column, multiple columns, or even the whole dataset.

To use the Data Validation Tool, go to the "Data" tab on the Excel toolbar and click on the "Data Validation" button. This will open a window with different validation choices.

Choose the Validation Rule: In the dialog box, describe the rule you want to use. For example, you can make a rule that only allows integers, dates within a certain range, or text of a certain length.

Define the Validation Criteria: Set the settings for the validation rule you have chosen, such as the minimum and maximum values, the range of dates, or the list of values that are allowed.

Customize the Error Alert: In Excel, you can show an error message when the user enters data that doesn't follow the validity rule. You can change this message to give the user instructions or more information.

Implement Data Validation: Click the "OK" button to apply the data validation to the range of cells you picked. Excel will stop you from entering data that doesn't fit the parameters you set.

Data Cleaning:

Eliminate Duplicates: If your dataset has duplicate records, Excel has a feature that lets you find and get rid of duplicate rows. Select the range of cells with your data and go to the "Data" tab. Click on the "Remove Duplicates" button and choose the columns to look at for duplicates. Excel will get rid of the duplicate rows and keep only the unique records.

Excel lets you split and merge data across multiple columns. For example, if you have a column with full names, you can split it into separate columns for first names and last names. To do this, select the column, go to the "Data" tab, click on the "Text to Columns" button, and follow the instructions in the wizard.

By using these features, you can improve the quality and integrity of your dataset. Data validation makes sure that your data meets certain standards, and data cleaning helps you get rid of duplicate records and reorganize your data so that you can analyze it better.

Statistical analysis is a powerful tool in Excel that lets you learn a lot from your data. With Excel's built-in statistical functions, you can find the mean, median, mode, standard deviation, and variance. These functions are the backbone of data analysis in Excel and help you quickly summarize and interpret your data.

Know Your Data: Before starting a statistical analysis, it's important to know your data well. Figure out the factors you want to look at and make sure they are in the right columns or rows.

Identify the Useful Statistical Functions: Excel comes with a large number of statistical functions that can be used for different kinds of analysis. Some of the most common functions are AVERAGE, SUM, COUNT, MIN, MAX, STDEV.S, VAR.S, and MEDIAN.

Use the Statistical Functions: Once you've found the right functions for your analysis, you can start using them on your dataset. Choose the cell where you want to show the result and enter the function using the function wizard or by typing it directly. For example, to find the average of a range of numbers, you can use the AVERAGE function: "=AVERAGE(A1:A10)".

Tune the Function Parameters: Each statistical function may need you to specify certain parameters, such as the range of cells or the number of arguments. You can change these parameters to fit your data and analysis needs. Excel will give you prompts and ideas to help you choose the right parameters.

After you use the statistical functions, Excel will calculate the desired measures for your data. Take some time to understand the results and think about what they mean. For example, the mean (average) gives you an idea of how your data tends to be, while the standard deviation shows how spread out or variable your data is.

Visualize the Results: Excel gives you a number of charting options to help you see your data and statistical analysis results. Creating charts helps you explain your findings more clearly, spot trends, and compare different variables.

Excel's What-If Analysis and Goal Seeking functions are powerful ways to look at different scenarios and results. What-If Analysis lets you change the values in your data and see what happens. Let's learn how to use these features in Excel 2024.

Analysis of "What If"

Excel's What-If Analysis lets you compare different scenarios by using data tables. To make a data table, put the different input numbers in one row or column of your spreadsheet and the formulas you want to look at in the cells next to them.

Apply the What-If Analysis: Go to the "Data" tab on the Excel bar and click the "What-If Analysis" button. From the dropdown menu, choose "Data Table." A dialog box will appear where you can set the row input cell and column input cell.

Interpreting the Results: Once the data table is made, you can see how changing the input values changes the results of your formulas. This is a powerful way to compare different scenarios and find the best solutions.

Goal Seeking

Define the Desired Outcome: Setting goals starts with figuring out what you want to happen. Find the cell with the formula you want to use and the desired outcome.

To use Goal Seeking, go to the "Data" tab on the Excel ribbon and click the "What-If Analysis" button. From the dropdown menu, choose "Goal Seek." A dialog box will appear where you can set the set cell (the cell with the formula), the to value (the desired result), and the by changing cell (the input cell to change).

Read the Results: Excel will change the value in the input cell until it finds a value that makes the formula result match the desired result. This is a useful tool for figuring out what inputs are needed to reach a certain goal.

If you know how to use Excel's What-If Analysis and Goal Seeking features, you can make better decisions by comparing different possible outcomes and finding the best answers.

Visualizing data in Excel is a powerful way to share information and insights. Excel's extensive charting features let you turn your raw data into visually appealing and useful charts.

Chapter 7: Visualizing Data Brilliance: Using Charts in Excel

A chart in Excel 2024 is a potent tool that enables you to visually depict your data, thereby simplifying comprehension and analysis. By plotting data points on a graph, charts assist us in spotting trends, patterns, and correlations within our data. When interpreting a chart, it's crucial to understand its various components, as they deliver valuable information about the represented data.

Starting with the chart's axes, the x-axis or the horizontal axis stands for the categories or values that are being measured. It provides the scale and labels for the data points along this axis. The y-axis, also called the vertical axis, signifies the numerical values being measured, offering the scale and labels for the data points along this axis. By scrutinizing the intersection of data points on the chart and their corresponding positions on the axes, we can achieve a deeper understanding of the relationship between variables.

The data points in a chart are represented by markers, bars, lines, or other graphical elements, based on the type of chart chosen. For instance, in a line chart, data points are linked by lines to exhibit trends over time. In a bar chart, data points are depicted by vertical or horizontal bars to compare values across categories. These visual representations facilitate the identification of highs, lows, and patterns within the data.

To enhance understanding, charts in Excel 2024 include a chart title, which gives a concise description of what the chart stands for. It aids viewers in quickly understanding the main concept or theme of the chart. Furthermore, legends are used to explain the meanings of different colors or symbols used in the chart. Legends play a pivotal role in clarifying the representation of various data series or categories within the chart.

Understanding the components of a chart and their significance can allow you to analyze and interpret the information displayed effectively. The axes, data points, chart title, and legends collectively convey insights and trends within your data. Thus, the next time you encounter a chart in Excel 2024, pay heed to these components to fully harness the power of visual data analysis.

In the following sections of this chapter, we will delve into the step-by-step procedure of creating and editing charts in Excel 2024. By honing these skills, you will be able to convert your raw data into visually appealing and informative charts. Let's embark on the thrilling journey of chart creation and explore the limitless possibilities for data visualization in Excel 2024.

How to create a Chart in Excel 2024

Constructing a chart in Excel 2024 is an intriguing and user-friendly process, even for novices. By adhering to a few straightforward steps, you can turn your raw data into visually striking and informative charts.

Firstly, you need to select the data you want to incorporate in the chart. This step involves highlighting the cells containing the data. For example, suppose you have a sales data table with columns for different product categories and respective sales figures for each category. You would select the cells covering this data range.

Having selected the data, navigate to the "Insert" tab in the Excel ribbon, located at the top of the Excel window. The "Insert" tab is where you can find an array of chart types to choose from. Excel provides a range of chart types, including column charts, line charts, pie charts, bar charts, and more. Select the chart type that best suits your data and visualization needs.

Once you've chosen a chart type, Excel will generate a basic chart based on the selected data. However, the chart isn't complete yet. It requires customization to make it more meaningful and visually attractive. Thankfully, Excel provides an array of options to modify and enhance your chart.

One crucial step in customizing your chart is adding titles. Titles offer a clear and brief description of what your chart represents. To add a title, select the chart and navigate to the "Chart Tools" section in the Excel ribbon. Click on the "Chart Title" button and choose the desired title option, such as "Above Chart" or "Centered Overlay Title". Enter a descriptive title that accurately represents the purpose of your chart.

Axis labels are another critical component of a chart. They provide context and assist viewers in understanding the scale and meaning of the data. Excel automatically generates axis labels based on the selected data, but you can customize them to suit your needs. To modify axis labels, select the chart and navigate to the "Chart Tools" section. Click on the "Axis Titles" button and choose the desired option. You can choose to add titles to the primary horizontal axis, the primary vertical axis, or both. Type in your desired labels to provide more context to your chart. You can add labels such as "Product Categories" or "Sales Figures" to provide clarity and understanding.

Data labels serve as an important customization feature in Excel graphs. They provide the capacity to demonstrate the precise values of data points within the graph. This feature is particularly handy when you need to highlight certain data points or offer accurate details to your audience. To incorporate data labels, select the graph and head to the "Chart Tools" tab. Tap on the "Data Labels" button and opt for the label option that suits your needs, such as showing values, percentages, or a combination of both.

Once you have tailored the chart elements to your preference, you have the opportunity to further finesse its visual aspect by altering colors, styles, and other aesthetic attributes. Excel furnishes a plethora of options to assure that your graph corresponds with your chosen style or fits your branding guidelines.

Modifying a graph in Excel 2024 provides an exhilarating chance to augment its visual appeal and underline key data points. By leveraging Excel's multifaceted editing features, you can improve the look of your graph and render it more impactful.

One technique to enrich your graph is by integrating lines, shapes, or text boxes. These components can be utilized to draw attention to certain data points or offer additional context. For instance, suppose you have a line graph depicting the sales performance of various products over a span of time. By integrating a vertical line at a specific date, you can underscore an important event or milestone that influenced sales. Similarly, shapes or text boxes can be employed to offer explanations or annotations within the graph, simplifying the data understanding for viewers.

Altering the colors and styles of graph components is another efficient way to boost the visual appeal of your graph. Excel presents a vast array of formatting options, enabling you to tailor the color schemes, fonts, and effects to accommodate your tastes or comply with your company's branding. For example, you can alter the color of the graph's background, modify the hues of the data series, or adjust the font size and style of the axis labels. These formatting options provide you with the versatility to create visually captivating graphs that are consistent and aligned with your overall presentation or report.

Excel also incorporates interactive features that allow users to engage with the graph and examine the data in greater detail. For example, you can activate data labels that display the exact values of the data points when hovered over. This enables viewers to attain specific information about each data point without overloading the graph with excessive labels. Moreover, you can include tooltips to offer additional information or insights when specific components of the graph are chosen. These interactive features render your graph more engaging and aid in a deeper comprehension of the underlying data.

Beyond these editing capabilities, Excel provides advanced charting options like 3D graphs, stacked graphs, and combination graphs. These options enable you to present your data in inventive and visually appealing manners, allowing you to effectively communicate complex information.

Summarize your data: In the "Values" area of the PivotTable Field List, you can decide how you want to summarize your data. For instance, you can choose the "Sum" function to compute the total sales amount, or opt for "Count" to ascertain the number of entries. Excel presents a variety of aggregation functions, such as average, minimum, maximum, and others. Select the appropriate function for each field based on the type of data you're examining.

Customize your pivot table: Excel furnishes various options to customize the appearance and behavior of your pivot table. You can alter the layout, apply filters to display specific data, change the formatting, and add calculations. These options enable you to tailor the pivot table to your specific analysis requirements.

Create a line chart: Once you've created your pivot table, you can generate a line chart to visualize the summarized data. Simply select the data within the pivot table that you want to include in the chart, head to the "Insert" tab, and choose the desired line chart type. Excel will automatically generate the chart based on your selected data, providing a visual representation of the trends and patterns.

By using pivot tables and line charts together, you can gain profound insights into your data. Pivot tables enable you to group and summarize your data based on different criteria, while line charts provide a visual representation of the summarized data over time. This combination assists you in identifying trends, comparing different categories, and uncovering hidden patterns that may not be evident from the raw data alone.

Most used charts in excel 2024

In Excel 2024, you have access to a wide variety of chart types that cater to different data visualization requirements. Understanding the various chart types and their appropriate usage is crucial for effectively communicating your data analysis. Let's delve into some of the most employed chart types in Excel:

Bar charts: Bar charts, including column and stacked bar charts, are ideal for comparing different categories or values. Column charts display data as vertical bars, while stacked bar charts allow for the comparison of subcategories within a main category. Bar charts are commonly used to showcase sales figures, project timelines, or survey responses. For instance, if you want to compare the sales performance of different regions, a column chart can help visualize the sales amounts for each region side by side.

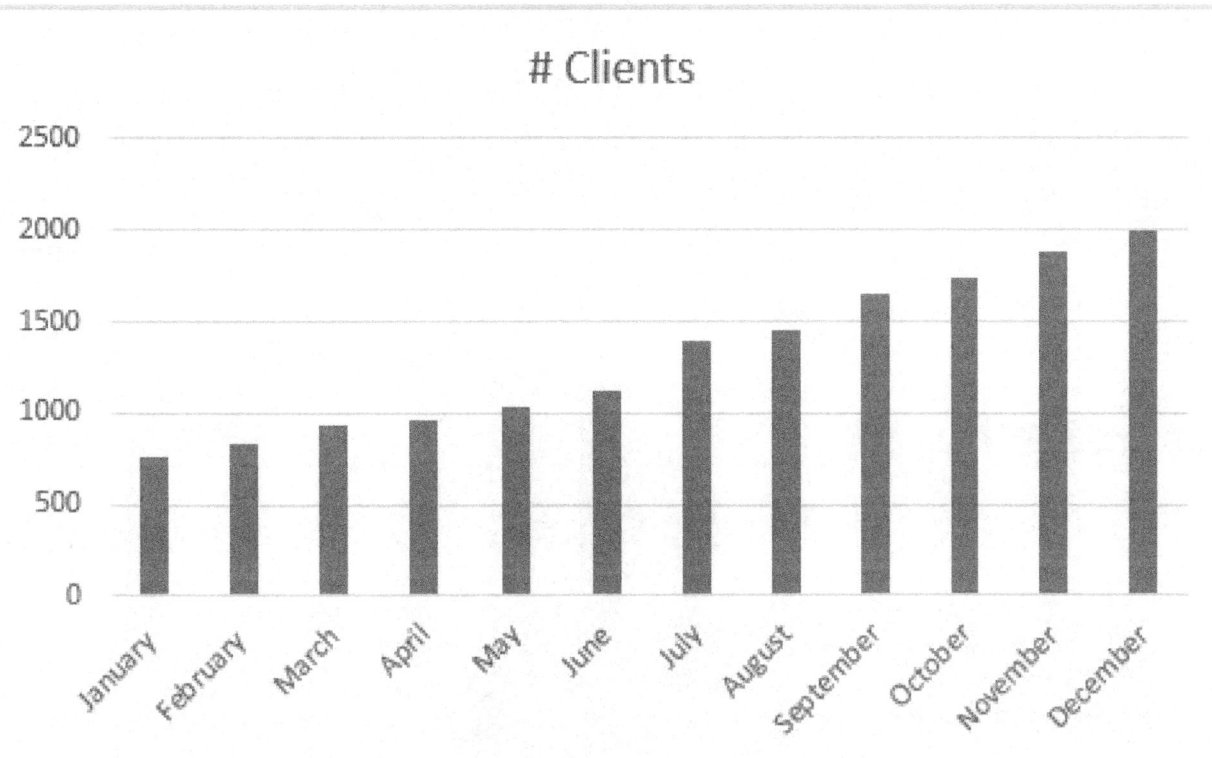

Bubble charts: Bubble charts are an extension of scatter plots that incorporate a third variable. They represent data points as bubbles, where the size of the bubble represents the value of the third variable. Bubble charts are effective in visualizing three-dimensional data relationships. For example, if you have data on the population, GDP, and area of different countries, a bubble chart can showcase the relationships between these variables.

Pie charts: Pie charts are excellent for depicting proportions and percentages. They are frequently used to represent market shares, budget allocations, or survey results. Each category is represented as a slice of the pie, with the size of the slice proportional to the value it represents. For example, if you have sales data for different products, a pie chart can help visualize the percentage contribution of each product to the total sales.

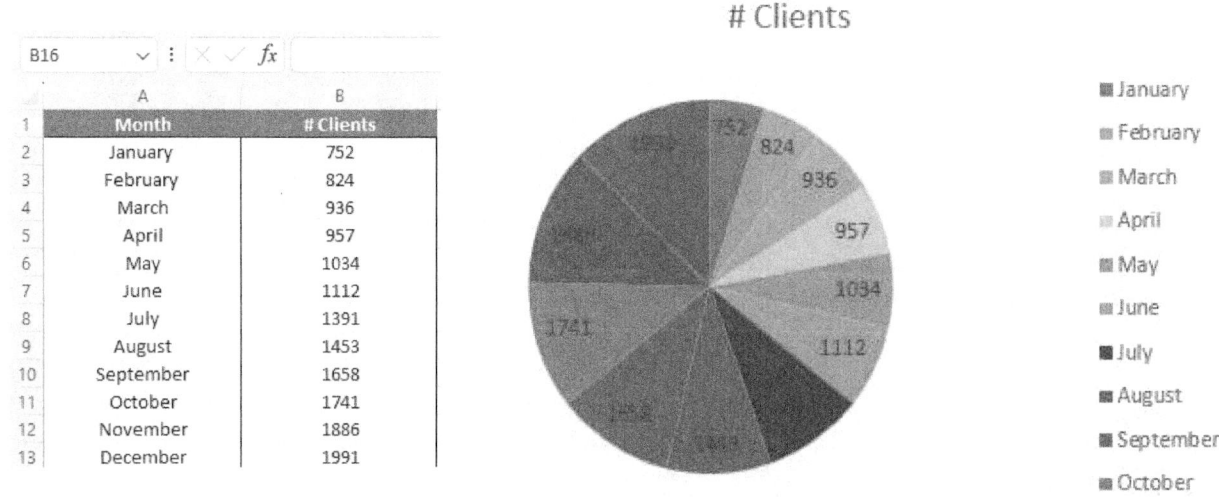

Line charts: Line charts are great for showing trends and changes over time. They are commonly used to track stock prices, monitor project progress, or analyze temperature variations. Line charts connect data points with straight lines, allowing you to observe patterns and fluctuations. For example, if you have monthly sales data, a line chart can help visualize the overall sales trend over the course of a year.

Scatter plots: Scatter plots are valuable for displaying relationships between two or more variables. They are particularly useful in analyzing correlations and identifying outliers. Each data point is represented as a dot on the chart, with one variable plotted on the x-axis and another on the y-axis. Scatter plots are commonly used in scientific research, financial analysis, and experimental data analysis.

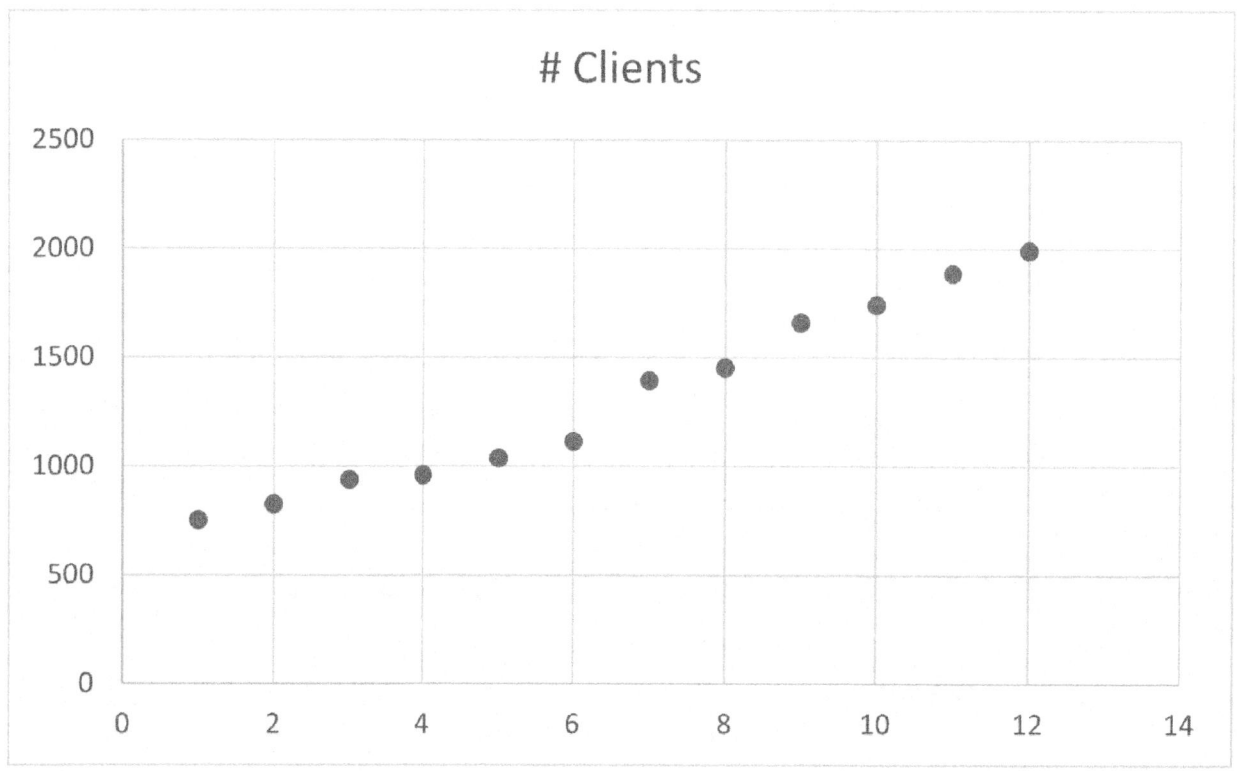

Choosing the right type of chart relies on the kind of data you have and the story you want to tell. Think about what your data looks like and what lessons you want to highlight. Try out different types of charts to find the one that shows your data best and gets your message across most clearly.

Chapter 8: Organize Like a Pro: Tables in Excel

In this chapter, we'll learn more about Excel 2024 tables. Tables are a powerful tool that can help you organize, analyze, and handle your data in a better way. For beginners who want to improve their Excel skills, it's important to know how tables work and how to use them. So, let's jump in and start looking at the Excel tables.

Understanding Why and How Tables Are Useful

In Excel, tables are a way to store and manage data in an organized way. They have many benefits, such as making it easier to enter data, making it easier to analyze data, and making it easier to style data on the fly. With tables, you can put your data in rows and columns, which makes it easier to track, filter, and group. Formulas and functions are also easier to use with tables because they change right away when new data is added. By using tables, you can make it easier to handle your data and speed up your work.

	A	B	C	D	E
1		An Excel Table			
2					
3		Year	Month	Clients	
4		2023	January	752	
5		2023	February	824	
6		2023	March	936	
7		2023	April	957	
8		2023	May	1034	
9		2023	June	1112	
10		2023	July	1391	
11		2023	August	1453	
12		2023	September	1658	
13		2023	October	1741	
14		2023	November	1886	
15		2023	December	1991	
16					

Everything you need to know about tables in excel 2024

Cleaning up our Dataset: Before we make a table, we need to make sure that our data is clean and well-organized. This includes getting rid of any rows or columns that aren't needed, fixing any spelling problems, and making sure the data is the same all over the dataset. Cleaning up your dataset will help you keep the purity of your data and avoid problems when working with tables.

Making a table in Excel: We can make a table in Excel in two different ways. The first option is to select the range of cells that hold our data and then click the "Insert Table" the button on the Ribbon. Excel will immediately turn the range into a table when it sees it. The second way is to use a computer shortcut. Press Ctrl + T, and Excel will request you to confirm the range that you wish to convert into a table.

Naming the Table: Once the table is made, it's best to give it a name that makes sense. This makes it easy to make formulas and VBA scripts that use the table. To give the table a name, click on it, go to the Table Design tab on the Ribbon, and type a name in the Table Name box.

Parts of an Excel Table: A table in Excel is made up of many different parts. The table is made up of columns, and each column has its own title. We can use the column titles to refer to the columns when doing calculations or filtering the data. The rows of the table show each record or entry. Each cell in the table has information about the meeting of a column and a row.

Table Design: Excel gives you a variety of choices for table design so you can change how your table looks. You can quickly change the format of your table by choosing from a list of standard table styles. You can also change things like the font style, cell borders, and background colors for each table section. You might be able to make your data easier to look at and understand if you try out different table styles.

Formatting the Table: Formatting is important to make your table easier to read and look better. Formatting options include making headers bold, highlighting certain rows or columns, and using conditional formatting to show data patterns or values that meet certain criteria. Setting up your table correctly can help you find trends, outliers, and important data points.

Entering Data into the Table: One benefit of using tables is that they make it easier to add data. To add data into a table, start putting in the column's last cell. Excel immediately makes the table bigger to fit the new row of data. This keeps you from having to change the data range by hand. To make a new row quickly, press Tab from the last cell in the table.

Data Validation in an Excel Table: With data validation, you can choose what kind of information can be put in each cell. This is helpful for keeping the info correct and preventing mistakes. To add data validation to a table, first select the range of cells you want to change, then go to the Data tab in the Ribbon and click the Data Validation button. You will see a dialog box where you can choose the validation criteria, such as whole numbers, times, or custom formulas.

Removing Data Validation: To remove data validation from a table, select the group of cells that have validation, go to the Data tab in the Ribbon, click the Data Validation button, and choose the "Clear All" option. This will remove all data validation criteria from the range you picked.

Returning an Excel Table to a Range: To return an Excel table to a range, select any cell in the table, go to the Table Design tab in the Ribbon, and click the "Convert to Range" box. Excel will return the table to a normal range while keeping the data and formatting.

Sorting and filtering data in Excel tables: Excel tables have features that make it easy to organize and evaluate data. These features are ordering and filtering. To sort data in a table, click on any cell in the table, go to the Table Design tab in the Ribbon, and then click the "Sort" button. It is possible to sort by one or more columns, either going up or down. To filter the information in a table, click on the filter icon in the top row of the column you want to filter.

Resizing Excel Tables: To change the size of an Excel table, select a cell in the table, go to the Table Design tab in the Ribbon, and drag the handle in the bottom right corner of the table to change the range. This lets you add and take away rows and columns from the table on the fly.

Changing the Design Style of an Excel Table: To change the design style of an Excel table, select any cell in the table, go to the Table Design tab in the Ribbon, and choose a different table style from the list. This quickly changes the way your table looks without changing the data.

Using the Excel Table Slicer: Slicers are a good way to organize data in Excel tables in a way that looks good. They have buttons that you can use to filter data quickly based on certain factors. To add a slicer to a table, click on any cell in the table, go to the Table Design tab in the Ribbon, and click the "Insert Slicer" button. Choose the column(s) you want to filter, and Excel will make a slicer box that lets you decide how the data in the table is displayed.

Pivot tables user manual

Excel's pivot tables are a powerful tool that let you sum up and examine a huge amount of data. They give you a flexible and active way to turn raw data into useful insights. By arranging and combining data based on different factors, pivot tables let you look for trends, patterns, and correlations in your data set.

To make a pivot table from an Excel table, follow these steps:

Pick a cell from the Excel table.

- Click on the "Insert" tab in the Ribbon.
- Click the "PivotTable" button.

Excel will ask you to check the range of the table. The full Excel table should be added to the area by default. After picking a range, you can say where you want the pivot table to go, such as on a new or a current worksheet.

When you make the pivot table, a list of PivotTable Fields will show up. This field list has all of the column names from your Excel table. To start looking at the data, put the fields in the PivotTable Field List into the Rows, Columns, Values, and Filters sections.

Let's say you have a sales data table in Excel with fields for Product, Region, Month, and Sales Amount. You want to look at total sales by area and by month. To make a pivot table, do the following:

- Drag the "Region" field from the PivotTable Field List to the Rows area.
- Move the "Month" field to the part called "Columns."
- Move the "Sales Amount" field to the part that says "Values."
- Based on the fields you choose, Excel will instantly add up the sales amount. You should now have a pivot table with the total sales for each month and area.

You can just drag and drop the fields in the PivotTable Field List to change the order of the groups in a pivot table. Drag the "Month" field to a different spot in the field list, for example, to change the order of the months in the column area.

The numbers in a pivot table can also be used in a variety of calculations. By default, Excel adds up the numbers, but you can change this to do other things, like average, count, minimum, maximum, and so on. Here's what you need to do to change the summary function:

- Click the drop-down arrow next to the field name in the Values area.
- Select "Value Field Settings" from the drop-down menu.
- Choose the summary feature you need from the list.

For example, choose "Average" in the Value Field Settings to see the average sales amount instead of the total.

You can also use pivot tables to sort and divide your data so that you can look at it in a more focused way. By adding new fields to the Filters box, you can make filters that do things. For example, to look at sales data for a certain product, add the "Product" field to the Filters area and select the product from the drop-down menu.

Design the pivot table. Once you have embedded the pivot table, you will see the PivotTable Field List. This is where you make your pivot table and change how it looks. On the right side of the screen, you'll see a list of the fields you can use from the data you've chosen. To set up the layout of your pivot table, drag and drop the fields you want into the "Rows," "Columns," and "Values" boxes.

You can also style and change the look of your pivot table to make it look better and make it easier to read. Excel has many formatting choices, such as the ability to highlight certain data points or trends by using different styles, fonts, colors, and conditional formatting.

With pivot tables, you can change the order and organization of your data by dragging and moving fields in the PivotTable Field List. This lets you look at data from different angles and from different points of view without changing the original information.

As you get better at using pivot tables, you can try out more complicated features like calculated fields and calculated items. You can use these tools in a pivot table to do complicated math and make new groups. For example, you could use a calculated field to figure out profit rates based on sales and costs.

Overall, if you want to analyze data in Excel, you need to be able to use pivot tables. You can use them to summarize, examine, and see data in a way that is interactive and flexible. If you know how to use pivot tables, you can get useful information and explain your results to others.

To make a copy of an Excel table, select the whole table (including the heads), press Ctrl+C, and then press Ctrl+V to paste it somewhere else. Excel will make a copy of the table, keeping the same data, layout, and functions.

Getting rid of an Excel table: If you no longer need an Excel table and want to turn it into a normal range, select any cell in the table, go to the Table Design tab in the Ribbon, and click the "Convert to Range" button. This gets rid of the table's style and features, but keeps the data.

Structured references make it easier to use table data in formulas. Instead of using cell references (like A1:B10), structured references use the table column headings to point to specific data areas in the table.

When a Formula Refers to the Whole Excel Table:

You can use the name of the table to refer to the full Excel table in a calculation. For example, if your table is called "SalesTable," you can use the phrase "=SalesTable" to refer to the whole table.

When a Formula Refers to the Data Part of an Excel Table:

For the data part of an Excel table, you can use the "@" sign followed by the column title name in a formula. Use the method "=SUM(SalesTable[@Amount])" to find out how much the "Amount" column in the table adds up to.

When an Excel formula refers to the table totals for a specific row:

If your table has a total row, you can use the name of the table and the column header name in a formula to refer to the total number for a certain column. For example, if your table is called "SalesTable" and you want to find the total amount in the "Amount" column, you can use the method "=SalesTable[[#Totals],[Amount]]".

When an Excel formula refers to the table totals for a certain column:

In the same way, you can use the structured reference formula with the column name in square brackets to talk about the table totals for a certain column. "=Table1[[Total],[Revenue]]" for example, refers to the total amount of income in Table1's Revenue column.

Referring to table totals in your formulas is a quick way to add combined data to your calculations and do analysis based on the summed up information.

Make sure to change the names of the table and columns as needed in your models. When you use the table totals feature, you can quickly view and use the data in your Excel table that has been put together to do more analysis and make decisions.

By learning how to use tables in Excel 2024, you get an important tool for organizing, analyzing, and showing data. Tables provide an organized framework that makes it easier to do hard things, like cleaning and formatting data, doing math, filtering and sorting, or making pivot tables for in-depth analysis.

You now know how to find your way around Excel tables and make the most of their power. With each new task, you will learn new ways to organize and analyze data that will help you get better at it. Excel tables will become an important tool for making smart choices and getting great insights from data.

Chapter 9: Pitfall Patrol: Common Mistakes to Avoid in Excel

In this chapter we will seecommon mishaps and mistakes that Excel users often stumble upon. It starts by tackling the challenge of understanding and accurately implementing formulas and functions, shedding light on their structure and usage to avoid calculation errors.

It further discusses the crucial aspect of data validation, offering a step-by-step approach to setting up rules and restrictions that ensure data consistency. The chapter underscores the significance of proper organization and structure in managing Excel worksheets and files, offering practical advice on systematic formatting and file management.

Attention is also given to common Excel error messages, providing a deeper understanding of each and offering remedies to rectify these mistakes. The chapter wraps up by identifying potential pitfalls associated with certain Excel features such as cell merging, maintaining a tabular layout, date formatting, dependency on external links, formatting whole columns/rows, storing multiple records in one cell, and the implications of different file types.

Equippedexamples and precise instructions, this chapter is designed to help readers circumnavigate common pitfalls in Excel, paving the way for accurate data analysis and a smoother Excel experience.

Misinterpretation of Formulas and Functions

One of the most common mistakes beginners make in Excel is misinterpreting formulas and functions. Formulas and functions are essential for performing calculations and analyzing data accurately. However, constructing formulas correctly can be challenging for newcomers, resulting in incorrect calculations and misleading outcomes. To avoid this pitfall, it's crucial to understand the basic syntax and logic behind formulas and functions.

Learn the basic structure of formulas: Formulas start with an equal sign (=) and consist of operators, cell references, and functions. For example, the formula "=A1+B1" adds the values in cells A1 and B1.

Understand the purpose and usage of functions: Excel offers a wide range of built-in functions that perform specific calculations or tasks. For instance, the SUM function adds a range of values, and the AVERAGE function calculates the average of a range.

Reference the correct cells or ranges in your formulas: Cell references can be absolute (e.g., A1) or relative (e.g., A1). Absolute references stay fixed when copied to other cells, while relative references adjust based on the relative position of the formula.

Double-check your formulas and compare the output against expected results: If the results don't match your expectations, review your formula construction and ensure that you're using the correct functions and references.

Example: Let's say you have a worksheet with sales data in column A and expenses data in column B. To calculate the total profit in column C, you can use the formula "=A1-B1". By correctly constructing the formula and referencing the appropriate cells, you'll obtain accurate profit calculations.

Inadequate Validation of Data

Inadequate validation of data is another common mistake in Excel. Data validation ensures that the entered data meets specific criteria or restrictions, preventing inconsistencies and errors. To avoid this pitfall, Excel provides a data validation feature that allows you to set rules and constraints on data entry.

- Select the cell or range where you want to apply data validation

- Go to the "Data" tab in the Excel ribbon and click on the "Data Validation" button.
- In the Data Validation dialog box, specify the validation criteria.
-

For example, you can restrict input to numeric values within a certain range or allow only entries from a predefined list.

- Customize error messages to guide users when incorrect data is entered. You can provide clear instructions or explanations about the expected data format.
- Test the data validation by entering different values into the validated cells and observing how Excel responds.

Example: Suppose you have a worksheet for tracking employee ages, and you want to ensure that the entered ages are between 18 and 65. You can apply data validation to the "Age" column and set the criteria to allow values between 18 and 65. This ensures that only valid age entries within the specified range are accepted.

Poor Worksheet and File Organization

Poor organization of worksheets and files can lead to confusion and inefficiency. Establishing a structured approach to organizing your Excel workbooks is essential for easy navigation and efficient management of your data.

- Use meaningful and descriptive sheet names. Rename your worksheets to reflect their content or purpose. For example, use names like "Sales Data," "Expenses," or "Summary."
- Arrange related sheets in logical order. Consider the flow of data or analysis and organize the sheets accordingly. Grouping related sheets together improves readability and reduces confusion.
- Use consistent formatting and styling throughout your workbook. Apply the same font, font size, and colors to maintain a cohesive and professional look.

- Consider implementing a standardized folder structure for your Excel files. Create a main folder for your workbooks and subfolders for specific projects or categories. This makes it easier to locate and manage your files.

Example: Imagine you have an Excel workbook for financial analysis, including sheets for income statements, balance sheets, and cash flow statements. By using descriptive sheet names like "Income Statement," "Balance Sheet," and "Cash Flow Statement" and organizing them in the order they appear in the financial analysis process, you'll have a well-structured workbook.

Common Errors in Excel

Excel is known for its error messages that appear when something goes wrong with a formula or data. Understanding and addressing these common errors is essential for maintaining accuracy in your Excel work.

- Familiarize yourself with common Excel errors. Some frequently encountered errors include the "####" error, "#DIV/0!", "#N/A", "#NAME?", "#NULL!", "#REF!", "#VALUE!", and "#NUM!". Each error signifies a specific issue.
- Review your formulas for errors. Check for incorrect cell references, divide by zero errors, invalid formula names, or inconsistencies in your formulas.
- Validate your data inputs. Ensure that your data entries are correct and match the expected format. For example, if you're performing calculations with dates, ensure that the dates are entered correctly and recognized by Excel as dates.
- Address errors by making the necessary corrections. Adjust your formulas, verify your cell references, or fix any data inconsistencies.

Example: Suppose you have a formula that divides a value in cell A1 by the value in cell B1. If B1 contains zero, Excel will display the "#DIV/0!" error. To resolve this error, you can modify your formula to include an IF statement that checks if B1 is zero and provides an alternative result or error message.

Pitfalls in Cell Merging, Non-Tabular Layout, Date Formatting, External Links, Formatting Whole Columns/Rows, Multiple Records in One Cell, and File Types

Excel offers various features that, if misused, can lead to pitfalls in data analysis, sorting, filtering, and collaboration. It's essential to understand these pitfalls and use the features appropriately.

- Avoid excessive cell merging. While merging cells can be useful for formatting purposes, excessive merging can complicate data manipulation and cause challenges in sorting and filtering.

- Ensure a tabular layout for your data. Excel works best with data arranged in tables, where each column represents a specific attribute or variable, and each row represents a record or observation. This facilitates data analysis and allows for efficient sorting and filtering.

- Use proper date formatting. When working with dates in Excel, ensure that they are formatted as dates and recognized by Excel as such. This enables accurate calculations, sorting, and filtering based on dates.

- Minimize reliance on external links. External links can create dependencies and potential errors in your workbooks. Whenever possible, consider consolidating data within a single workbook or updating external links to avoid broken references.

- Format only the necessary cells. Avoid formatting entire columns or rows unnecessarily, as this can slow down Excel and make your workbook larger than necessary. Apply formatting only to the cells that require specific styling or highlighting.

- Avoid storing multiple records in a single cell. Excel is not designed for storing multiple records within a single cell. Instead, use separate cells or columns to maintain data integrity and facilitate analysis.

- Save your work in the latest Excel file format. By saving your work in the latest file format (e.g., .xlsx), you can take advantage of all the features and improvements offered by Excel 2024.

Example: Let's say you have a worksheet where you need to display a summary of sales for each quarter. Instead of merging cells to create a large merged cell for the summary, create a table with separate cells for each quarter. This allows for easy data manipulation and analysis, such as sorting sales by quarter or calculating total sales for a specific period.

By following these step-by-step instructions and examples, you can avoid common mistakes in Excel and work more efficiently and accurately with your data. Remember to pay attention to formula construction, validate your data inputs, organize your worksheets and files properly, address common Excel errors, and use Excel features appropriately. With practice and familiarity, you'll become more proficient in Excel and achieve accurate and meaningful results in your data analysis.

Chapter 10: Excel Wizardry: Uncover Advanced Tricks

In this section, we will explore advanced techniques in Excel that aim to enhance productivity and save valuable time. These techniques are specifically designed for beginners, providing clear instructions and practical examples. By mastering these advanced tricks, you will gain confidence and efficiency in navigating Excel. The topics covered include adding a drop-down list, composing text using the "&" operator, hiding formulas and data, transposing values, inputting values starting with 0, performing vague searches using Excel's wildcard character, applying restrictions on input using data validation, and utilizing time-saving templates, freezing rows and columns, and transposing columns and rows.

Adding a drop-down list

One useful thing about Excel is that you can add a drop-down list, which reduces the choices in a cell to a set of options you've already chosen. This gets rid of the need to enter data by hand and makes sure that your files are all the same. By making a drop-down list, you can make it easier to enter data and reduce mistakes. For example, if you have a worksheet that asks users to choose a department from a list you've already made, you can quickly make a drop-down list of department names so that users can choose the right department from the list instead of typing it in by hand.

Follow these steps to add a drop-down list in Excel 2024:
- Choose the cell or group of cells where the drop-down list should show.
- Go to the Excel Ribbon tab and click on the "Data" tab.
- In the "Data Tools" group, click on the "Data Validation" button.
- Select "List" from the "Allow" drop-down choice in the "Data Validation" dialog box.
- In the "Source" field, you can either type in the numbers for your drop-down list or select a range of cells that contain the list.
- Click "OK" to apply the drop-down menu to the chosen cells.
- Now, when you click on a cell with a drop-down list, a small arrow will appear to

show that you can choose a value from the list. This makes it easier to enter data and makes sure that only correct choices are made.

How to Put Together Text with "&"

You can combine or join text strings from different rows or within a formula using the "&" operator in Excel. This is helpful if you need to mix text from different sources into a single cell or if you want to make labels or messages that change based on what is being typed.

Follow these steps to write text in Excel 2024 with the "&" operator:

- Choose the cell where you want the text to go.
- Start typing the text you want to include. When you want to add content from another cell, type "&" followed by the cell reference or range.
- Type the rest of the text, using the "&" operator whenever you need to bring in information from another space.
- Press Enter to finish writing the piece.

For example, let's say you have the first name in cell A2 and the last name in cell B2 and you want to make a full name in cell C2. You can join the first name and last name with the "&" function, like this: =A2&" "&B2. This will put a space between the names in cells A2 and B2, making the full name in cell C2.

Hiding Formulas

Hide formulas in Excel to protect private calculations or make your worksheet easier to read. By hiding formulas, you can make sure that users don't change the calculations underneath by mistake and give them a cleaner interface.

Here are the steps you need to take to hide formulas in Excel 2024:

- Choose the cells or set of cells where the formulas you want to hide are located.
- Right-click on the cells you want to change and choose "Format Cells" from the menu that appears.
- Go to the "Number" tab in the "Format Cells" box.
- Choose "Custom" from the list.
- Enter three semicolons (;;;) in the "Type" field to set up a custom format with no visible text.
- Click "OK" to make the changes.

Now, the formulas in the chosen cells will be hidden, and you will only be able to see the results of the calculations. This can be helpful if you want to show others a simplified version of your worksheet or keep your numbers accurate.

Keeping information secret

By hiding data in Excel, you can keep it private and make your files less cluttered. When you hide data, it goes away from the page and can't be seen. This can be very helpful when you have big datasets with lots of information that you don't always need to show.

Here are the steps you need to take to hide info in Excel 2024:

- Choose the cells or set of cells that you want to hide.
- Right-click on the cells you want to change, and then choose "Format Cells" from the menu that appears.
- Go to the "Protection" tab in the "Format Cells" box.
- Click on the "Hidden" box.
- Click "OK" to make the changes.

Now, the chosen cells won't show up, and neither will their contents. Note, though, that hiding data doesn't give you full security because the data can still be accessed by unhiding the cells or in other ways. To make Excel more secure, you might want to use password protection or other advanced security methods.

Transposing Values

By transposing numbers in Excel, you can change the way your data is laid out, turning rows into columns and columns into rows. This can be very helpful when you need to rearrange or restructure your data to make it fit a certain plan or analysis.

Follow these steps to change the order of numbers in Excel 2024:

- Choose the range of cells that you want to switch.
- Right-click on the cells you want to copy and pick "Copy" from the menu that appears.
- Choose the cell where you want the data to start being moved.
- Right-click on the cell and choose "Paste Special" from the menu that appears.
- Check the "Transpose" box in the "Paste Special" dialogue box.
- Click "OK" to put the change into effect.

Now, the chosen cells' rows will become columns or vice versa. This can be especially helpful when you have data set up in rows but need to show or examine it in columns.

Putting in numbers that start with 0

Excel may automatically get rid of leading zeros when working with numbers that start with 0. This can be a problem if the zeros are important to your data. To keep the beginning zeros, you need to format the cells as text.

Follow these steps to put in numbers that start with 0 in Excel 2024:

- Choose the cells where you want to start entering numbers with 0.
- Right-click on the cells you want to change, and then choose "Format Cells" from the menu that appears.
- Go to the "Number" tab in the "Format Cells" box.
- Choose the "Text" group.
- Click "OK" to make the changes.

Now, when you put numbers in the formatted cells that start with 0, Excel will treat them as text and keep the beginning zeros. This makes sure that your data is shown correctly and that the starting zeros are not taken away.

Use Excel's Wildcard Character to do a broad search

With Excel's "wildcard" character, you can do searches that aren't exact matches but are based on trends instead of exact matches. This can help if you're looking for specific trends in your data or if you only know part of what you need to know about the thing you're looking for.

Follow these steps to use the wildcard character in Excel 2024 to do a broad search:

- Click on the header of the cell or column where you want to look.
- When you press Ctrl+F on your computer, the "Find" box will appear.
- In the "Find What" field, type in the search pattern you want to use or the information you already know.
- If you want Excel to look for an exact match, check the "Match entire cell contents" box.
- Check the "Match case" box if you want Excel's search to take case into account.
- Click "Find Next" to begin looking.

Excel will look in the area you've chosen for the pattern or information you've given it, and the cells that match the search criteria will be highlighted. The "" character can stand for any number of characters, while the "?" character can only stand for one character. For example, if you type "App" in the "Find What" box, Excel will look for cells that start with "App" followed by any number of characters.

Using Data Validation to put limits on what can be typed in

Data checking lets you put limits on what kind of information can be put into a cell. This helps keep the data correct and stops users from adding wrong or inconsistent information.

Follow these steps to put data checking into place in Excel 2024:

- Choose the cell or area where you want to use data validation.
- Go to the Excel Ribbon and click on the "Data" tab.

- In the "Data Tools" group, click on the "Data Validation" button.
- In the "Data Validation" dialog box, you can choose the factors for validation based on your needs. You can, for example, choose to only accept whole numbers or a certain range of numbers.
- Change the input message and error alert message to tell people what to do and give them feedback.
- Click "OK" to validate the info.

Now, when users try to enter data into the verified cell or range, Excel will check the data against the criteria you set and show an error message if the data doesn't meet the requirements. This makes sure that only true data is put into your worksheets, so mistakes and inconsistencies are less likely to happen.

One click is all it takes to get more status

Without having to use complicated formulas, the Status Bar in Excel can quickly summarize or calculate chosen data. This lets you get ideas and do math on the spot, which saves you time and work.

Follow these steps to get more state information from the state Bar in Excel 2024:

- Choose the set of data about which you want to know the state.
- Check the Status Bar, which is in the bottom right area of the Excel window.
- When you right-click on the Status Bar, a list of summary features like Sum, Count, Average, Minimum, and Maximum will appear.
- Pick the summary function you want from the list.

Excel will quickly figure out and show in the Status Bar the chosen summary function for the selected data range. This gives you a quick look at important information without requiring you to write complicated numbers or use extra cells for calculations.

Time-Saving Templates

Excel 2024 has a lot of templates that have already been made, which can save you a lot of time when working on common jobs or projects. These templates are ready-to-use spreadsheets for budgets, calendars, invoices, job plans, and other things. By using these templates, you can get your work started quickly and change them to fit your needs.

Follow these steps to find templates that will save you time in Excel 2024:

- Click on the "File" tab in the Ribbon when Excel is open.
- To open the "New Workbook" pane, choose "New" from the menu on the left.
- In the "New Workbook" pane, you'll find a number of template types, such as "Budgets," "Calendars," "Planners," and more.
- You can look through the themes or use the search bar to find the one you want.
- When you click on a template, you can see a sample and read about it.
- Once you've chosen a template, click "Create" to open a new workbook based on that design.

You can use the template to get worksheets, formulas, and formatting that are already set up for the job or project. Then, you can change the template to fit your needs by adding your own data, making changes to the formulas, and changing the style. This saves you time and effort when setting up your workbook's structure and formatting, so you can focus on the real content and analysis.

By adding these advanced tricks to your Excel routine, you can get things done faster, save time, and improve your ability to analyze data. From adding drop-down lists and combining text with the "&" operator to hiding formulas and data, transposing values, using data validation, taking advantage of time-saving templates, freezing rows and columns, and transposing columns and rows, these tips will help you work smarter and get the most out of Excel 2024. With practice and research, you will find even more ways to use Excel to improve your work and get great results.

Conclusion: Life's Solutions, Excel Style: Solve Everyday Problems with Excel

In this concluding chapter, we will delve deeper into how Excel can be utilized to solve everyday problems and enhance various aspects of our lives. While Excel is commonly known for its data analysis and financial modeling capabilities, it is essential to recognize that it is a versatile software that can significantly impact personal finances, career development, and general problem-solving. As we approach the end of our Excel journey, we will focus on two key areas where Excel can make a difference: improving personal finances and its broader impact on lives and careers.

Learn How to Improve Personal Finances

Excel provides a robust platform for effectively managing personal finances, budgeting, and tracking expenses. By leveraging its wide array of functions and features, you can gain better control over your financial situation and make informed decisions regarding spending, saving, and investing. Let's explore some step-by-step actions you can take using Excel to improve your personal finances:

Create a Personal Budget: Begin by setting up a comprehensive budget spreadsheet in Excel to monitor your income and expenses. Enumerate all sources of income and categorize your expenses, such as rent/mortgage, utilities, groceries, transportation, entertainment, and savings. Excel's built-in formulas can aid in calculating totals and analyzing your spending habits.

- Example: Create a budget spreadsheet where you list your monthly income and categorize expenses. Use the SUM function to calculate the total income and expenses, and use conditional formatting to highlight areas where you may be overspending.

PERSONAL BUDGET

2023

REVENUE	JAN	FEB	MAR	APR	MAY	JUN	JUL	AUG	SEP	OCT	NOV	DEC	YEAR
INCOME													
Wages	$2.600,00	$2.600,00	$2.600,00										$7.800,00
Interest/Dividends	$649,00	$313,00	$664,00										$1.626,00
Miscellaneous	$474,00	$643,00	$380,00										$1.497,00
Total	$3.723,00	$3.556,00	$3.644,00	$0,00	$0,00	$0,00	$0,00	$0,00	$0,00	$0,00	$0,00	$0,00	$10.923,00

EXPENSES	JAN	FEB	MAR	APR	MAY	JUN	JUL	AUG	SEP	OCT	NOV	DEC	YEAR
HOME													
Mortgage	$750,00	$750,00	$750,00										$2.250,00
Insurance													$0,00
Repairs			$75,00										$75,00
Services	$35,00	$35,00	$35,00										$105,00
Utilities	$165,00	$165,00	$165,00										$495,00
Total	$950,00	$950,00	$1.025,00	$0,00	$0,00	$0,00	$0,00	$0,00	$0,00	$0,00	$0,00	$0,00	$2.925,00

Track Expenses: Maintain a record of your daily expenses using Excel. Create a separate sheet where you can input your expenses and categorize them accordingly. Excel's functions, such as SUM, COUNTIF, and charts, can assist in analyzing your spending patterns and identifying areas where you can cut costs.

- Example: Create an expense tracker sheet where you enter the date, category, and amount spent for each expense. Use the SUMIF function to calculate the total expenses for each category and create a pie chart to visualize the distribution of expenses.

Plan for Savings and Investments: Utilize Excel to establish savings goals and monitor your progress. Create a dedicated sheet to track your savings and investments, and utilize Excel's financial functions to calculate compound interest over time. This will help you project future savings and investment growth.

- Example: Create a savings tracker where you input your savings goal, monthly contributions, and interest rate. Use the FV function to calculate the future value of your savings and monitor your progress towards your goal.

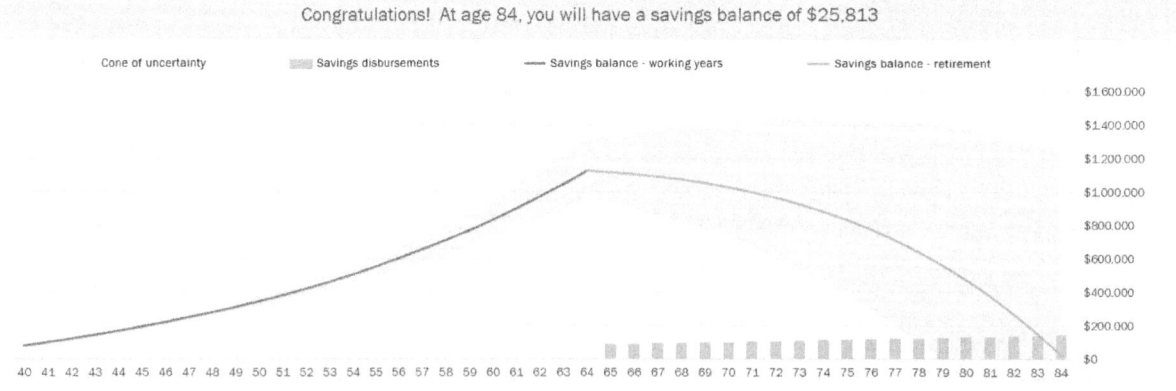

Analyze Debt and Loans: If you have debts or loans, Excel can assist you in creating repayment plans and analyzing interest rates and payment schedules. Utilize Excel's financial functions, such as PMT and IPMT, to calculate monthly payments and interest costs.

- Example: Set up a loan repayment calculator where you input the loan amount, interest rate, and loan term. Use the PMT function to calculate the monthly payment and the IPMT function to analyze the interest and principal portions of each payment.

Visualize Financial Data: Excel offers a range of charting options to visually represent your financial data. Create charts to compare expenses over time, track the growth of your investments, or monitor the proportion of income allocated to different expense categories. Visualizing data makes it easier to understand and identify trends or areas that require attention.

- Example: Create a line chart that shows your monthly expenses over a year. This allows you to identify months with higher expenses and make necessary adjustments.

By utilizing Excel's capabilities for personal finance management, you can gain better control over your money, make informed decisions, and work towards achieving your financial goals.

Excel's Impact on Lives and Careers

Excel has become an indispensable tool across various industries and professions. Its ability to efficiently organize and analyze data has transformed the way we work and make decisions. Let's explore some examples of how Excel has impacted lives and careers:

Finance and Accounting: Excel is extensively used in finance and accounting departments for financial analysis, budgeting, forecasting, and data reporting. It empowers professionals to handle complex financial calculations, automate repetitive tasks, and generate insightful reports.

- Example: Financial analysts use Excel to perform financial modeling, create cash flow statements, and analyze financial ratios.

Project Management: Excel's flexibility and project management capabilities have made it a go-to tool for planning, tracking progress, and analyzing project data. Project managers can create Gantt charts, track milestones, manage resources, and make data-driven decisions to ensure project success.

- Example: A project manager uses Excel to create a project timeline, assign tasks to team members, and monitor project progress through visual representations.

Sales and Marketing: Excel plays a vital role in sales and marketing by facilitating the management of customer data, analyzing sales trends, creating sales forecasts, and tracking marketing campaigns. It empowers professionals to identify opportunities, measure performance, and optimize strategies based on data insights.

- Example: A marketing analyst uses Excel to analyze customer data, segment the customer base, and create targeted marketing campaigns.

Human Resources: Excel simplifies various HR tasks, including managing employee data, tracking attendance, calculating payroll, and analyzing workforce metrics. It streamlines HR processes, improves accuracy, and enables data-driven decision-making in areas like recruitment, performance evaluation, and talent management.

- Example: An HR manager uses Excel to track employee attendance, calculate leave balances, and analyze employee performance metrics.

Education and Research: Excel is a valuable tool for educators, researchers, and students alike. It aids in data analysis, statistical calculations, and creating interactive models for educational purposes. Excel's versatility allows for the exploration of various subjects, from scientific research to financial modeling.

-
-
- Example: A researcher uses Excel to analyze survey data, perform statistical tests, and create visual representations of research findings.

Excel's impact extends far beyond these examples, as it has become a valuable asset in almost every industry. Regardless of your profession or career path, developing Excel skills can open doors to new opportunities, improve efficiency, and enhance your problem-solving capabilities.

In this comprehensive journey through Excel, we have covered a wide range of topics, from the basics for beginners to advanced tricks and techniques. As a reader, you have gained a solid understanding of Excel's interface, terminology, essential keyboard shortcuts, the power of formulas and functions, data analysis, visualization, organizing data with tables, common mistakes to avoid, and advanced tricks to enhance your efficiency. It's an impressive amount of information that you have acquired, and now it's time to put it all into practice.

Throughout this book, we have strived to present the material in a clear and accessible manner, tailored specifically for beginners with varying computer skills. We have avoided excessive theory, instead focusing on practical examples, step-by-step guides, and real-world scenarios. By taking this approach, we aimed to equip you with the necessary knowledge and skills to tackle everyday problems and make the most of Excel's capabilities.

You have learned how to navigate the Excel universe, mastering its terminology and essential keyboard shortcuts. You have witnessed the power of formulas and functions, enabling you to perform calculations, manipulate data, and uncover valuable insights. Data analysis has become second nature, as you have learned how to analyze data, interpret trends, and present findings with captivating graphs. The organization of data through tables has allowed you to effectively manage and structure your worksheets. You have also gained an awareness of common pitfalls to avoid, ensuring accuracy and integrity in your work. Furthermore, you have explored advanced tricks and techniques, broadening your Excel skills and unlocking new possibilities.

As you venture further into your journey with Excel, it is critically important to nurture a growth mindset, a mental approach that embraces challenges as opportunities for advancement rather than roadblocks halting your progress. With every challenge that arises, remember to perceive it not as a setback, but rather as a golden opportunity to broaden your understanding, refine your skills, and elevate your mastery of Excel.

Excel is not a static piece of software; it is a complex and continuously evolving tool, consistently enriched with new features and updates. This constant evolution makes it an endless landscape of learning and discovery. As such, there will always be new areas to explore, new features to master, and advanced functionalities to understand. The presence of the unfamiliar should not deter you but should motivate you to uncover these uncharted territories of knowledge and skills.

In light of this, maintaining an attitude of curiosity is key. Continue to question, explore, and delve into the depths of Excel's capabilities. The tool's true potential can only be fully realized when you continually seek to understand its evolving functionalities. If you encounter a feature or function you're unfamiliar with, don't hesitate to investigate. Leverage resources, ask questions, experiment, and through this process, you will expand your comprehension and proficiency in Excel.

This persistent pursuit of knowledge will not only contribute to your skillset but will also keep you on the cutting edge of Excel's advancements, ensuring you remain a competent and up-to-date user. By adopting this mindset, your journey with Excel will cease to be a static path and become a dynamic, enriching, and rewarding adventure.

Furthermore, you've successfully navigated the previously intimidating terrain of data analysis, transforming it from a daunting challenge into an intrinsic part of your toolkit. The once overwhelming waves of numbers and figures have become familiar friends, as you've honed your ability to analyze these elements, deriving meaning from the seemingly mundane.

You've not only learned how to parse data, but also to interpret subtle trends and patterns. The ability to spot a trend, to see a pattern unfold over time or to identify an outlier in an otherwise consistent data set, has become a second nature. You've developed an intuitive understanding of data that extends beyond the superficial, reaching into the depths of the story that the data is trying to tell.

Moreover, you've mastered the art of translating these abstract numerical narratives into compelling, tangible stories. Raw data, which may initially seem dry and unappealing, is now elegantly converted into engaging narratives that are presented through visually captivating graphs. These graphs not only make data more digestible, but also breathe life into numbers, making your findings resonate on a more human and understandable level.

In addition, you've gained command over the organization of data into structured tables, which are the backbone of effective data analysis in Excel. Understanding the power of tables, you've learned to arrange data systematically, structuring your worksheets in a way that fosters efficiency and enhances understanding. This skill has empowered you to manage vast volumes of data with ease, transforming seemingly chaotic arrays of information into well-organized, easily navigable structures.

This expertise has changed the way you work with Excel, making the process not just an exercise in data manipulation, but a means of telling powerful stories, making informed decisions, and discovering hidden insights. Indeed, the world of data analysis is now an open book for you to read, interpret, and leverage in myriad ways.

You have come a long way in your Excel journey. You have acquired the fundamental skills and knowledge needed to tackle everyday problems, analyze data, and make informed decisions. Remember that Excel is a versatile tool that can enhance various aspects of your personal and professional life. Embrace the confidence you have gained and put your newfound Excel expertise into practice. The possibilities are endless, and Excel is your ally in solving life's challenges with ease and efficiency. Excel style.

Printed in Great Britain
by Amazon